PROVERBS

Wisdom For All Ages

PROVERBS

Wisdom For All Ages

THOMAS L. SEALS

QUALITY PUBLICATIONS
P.O. BOX 1060
ABILENE, TEXAS 79604-1060

©Thomas L. Seals

ISBN: 0-89137-529-5

Table of Contents

6

8

Preface

Proverbs is truly wisdom for all ages. It is the one book in the Old Testament which gives practical advice on how to live godly lives in the midst of a changing world. It has no equal aside from the small epistle of James in the New Testament. For this reason, we have undertaken the task of writing this book in order to equip the man and woman of God with the wisdom of Proverbs. Through the application of such wisdom in our daily lives, we can be made better men and women of God and thus make a better society.

In studying this book, the reader will notice that we devote the opening chapter to a study of "Wisdom Literature." It is difficult to properly understand Proverbs without a basic knowledge of wisdom literature and Hebrew poetry. We have tried to make the study of wisdom literature scholarly, yet simple enough to be understood by the average reader. It is hoped that such emphasis will open up a new world of insight into the study and understanding of this great book of Hebrew wisdom.

Proverbs, Wisdom for All Ages is the conclusion of many months of labor and dreams. I first became acquainted with the wisdom of Proverbs when I was an undergraduate student at David Lipscomb College in Nashville, Tennessee. My professor, Dr. John Willis, now of Abilene Christian University, introduced me to this study and started me on a road that ends with the publication of this book. I am indebted to Dr. Willis for instilling within me a love for this Old Testament book as well as the basic outline which I am using in this publication.

In writing this book, I am indebted to others also. Over the past several years I have taught Proverbs to four or five Ladies' Bible Classes where I ministered. My basic outline has also been taught to several adult classes from time to time. In all of these classes I was encouraged by the response to the study and the kind remarks that suggested publication. I extend my gratitude to these classes and individuals who make studying and teaching God's word so enriching.

Finally, I am greatly indebted to my wife, Barbara, for her skill at the typewriter, for her diligence and tolerance, and for her love which tolerated several repeated classes on Proverbs. With such assistance and encouragement, I cannot but publish this work.

Thomas L. Seals

Introduction

INTRODUCTORY REMARKS

In any introductory material to the book of Proverbs, it is essential that some time be spent in studying what is called the Wisdom Movement in Israel. This movement produced that body of literature called Wisdom Literature. It is important to understand that much of the Old Testament is written in Hebrew poetry, a fact not well known due to the popularity of the King James Version Bible with its running verse. Most of Job, the Psalms, Proverbs, Lamentations, Ecclesiastes, and many sections of the prophetic books were written in Hebrew poetry. We do not wish to leave the impression, however, that the Wisdom Movement was original to Hebrew life. On the contrary, it was common to all cultures of the East and probably originated in foreign cultures. For example, we read concerning King Solomon:

> "And God gave Solomon wisdom and understanding beyond measure, and largeness of mind like the sand on the seashore, so that Solomon's wisdom surpassed the wisdom of all the people of the east, and all the wisdom of Egypt. For he was wiser than all other men, wiser than Ethan the Ezrahite, and Heman, Calcol, and Darda, the sons of Mahol; and his fame was in all the nations round about" (1 Kings 4:29-31).[1]

We know also that Job and his friends were of non-Israelite extraction. Then too, "Massa" of Proverbs 30:1 and 31:1 may reflect an Arabian milieu.[2] It was due to the international interest in

---

[1] Solomon's wisdom is further evidenced by the words of the queen of Sheba who was astonished by his wisdom (cf 1 Kings 10:1-7).

[2] "Massa," meaning "burden" or "oracle" might refer to the Arabian tribe of Massa mentioned in Gensis 25:14 and 1 Chronicles 1:30.

Wisdom Literature that a common interest among the nations developed which resulted in direct parallels of such literature in both Hebrew and pagan sources. It is important, therefore, that we understand Wisdom Literature in order to enrich our study of the book of Proverbs.

ORIGIN OF WISDOM LITERATURE

The ultimate origin of Wisdom Literature was in *common sense,* in the common observations of day to day life. Wisdom Literature, as a distinct body of writings, probably developed in the royal court where there was always a class of men in positions of educators, philosophers and advisors to train and develop young princes for government service. As a result of this, there arose a class of "wise" men, or sages, in the courts of Israel separate and apart from the prophets and priests. This distinction between prophet, priest and wise man is encountered in the book of Jeremiah. It seems that Jeremiah was considered a dangerous influence by some of the leading men in Jerusalem during his ministry. In fact, a plot was made against his life: "Come, let us make plots against Jeremiah, for the law shall not perish from the priest, nor counsel from the wise, nor the word from the prophet" (Jeremiah 18:18). Here is the indication that, along with the three-point division of the Hebrew Bible (Law, Prophets and Writings), there were also three types of authoritative guides: the priests, the prophets, and the wise men. Thus, the wise men were a kind of "third force" in the religious and social life of the people of the Old Testament.

As pointed out above, Wisdom Literature was not original to Hebrew life. It was common to all cultures of the East and much of Hebrew Wisdom is borrowed from other cultures.[3] This being true, the dating of the beginning of the Wisdom Literature movement in Israel would be at the time Israel had the greatest contact with the outside world. The peak of Israel's contact with the outside world came during the reign of Solomon, therefore, this is the date usually marked as the beginning of the Wisdom Literature age in Israel. This is not to say, however, that Wisdom Literature did not exist prior to this time in Israel, but that this was the time when it made its greatest impact on the nation.

---

[3]Charles T. Fritsch, *The Interpreter's Bible,* Volume 4, *Psalms, Proverbs* (Nashville, 1955), pp 767-69.

Before the Exile (587-539 BC), there were two main schools of writing in Israel: the Exodus/Sinai School and the Royal/Kingship School. The Exodus/Sinai School was emphasized in the northern kingdom of Israel, which rejected the kingship theology and urged a return to the covenant relationship enjoyed with God at the giving of the Law to Moses at Sinai. On the other hand, the Royal/Kingship School believed that God's covenant with his people was mediated through the king. This school was emphasized in the southern kingdom of Judah. After the Exile, however, there arose several different schools of theology. The four main schools were: Priestly, Messianism, Apocalyptic and Wisdom. A diagram of these various schools of thought may be drawn as follows:

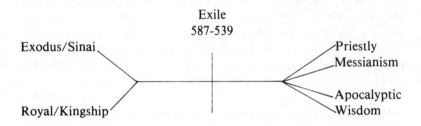

The Priestly School dedicated itself to keeping the Babylonian exiles in remembrance of the priestly system of worship and sacrifices utilized at the temple in Jerusalem. This was essential for in exile the children of God would tend to forget such a system of worship because there was no temple in Babylon. The Messianism School stressed nationalism. This School looked forward to the day when the Messiah would come, free the children of Israel from bondage and restore them to a position of leadership over the world. The Apocalyptic School stressed salvation at the end of time, not in history. As such, the Apocalyptic School thrived in any period of national disaster, such as the Babylonian Captivity. Finally, the Wisdom School stated that it was a mistake to look for God's relationship with his people on a cosmic or a national scale. This School taught that man must be concerned with the common, everyday relationship between man and God, man and man, and man and his environment. It was from this school of thought that works like Proverbs, Job and Ecclesiastes developed.

FORMS OF WISDOM LITERATURE

The Wisdom movement resulted in a religious philosophy, or a moral order, which had established itself through experience. The result was that a good man could find satisfaction in life. This satisfaction resulted from following rules and guideposts gleaned from experience in day to day life. This philosophy also provided rational and practical explanations of man's existence and his intellectual and moral problems.

In dealing with the practical problems of everyday life, the wise men immersed themselves into practically every experience in the world of human affairs. This immersion resulted in two forms of wisdom, the practical and the skeptical (also called speculative). The practical wisdom included literature like our present day book of Proverbs. It concerns the everyday problems and events of life and enjoins practical instructions as to how to cope with life, its problems and events. Skeptical wisdom is concerned with the question, "Why are things going so bad when I have been so good and have lived according to the proverbs of the righteous men?" It is represented in works like the books of Job and Ecclesiastes.

Wisdom literature sought to give to mankind a unified structural principle in life. In both the practical and skeptical literature, the wise men wrestled with life and its problems in an effort to enrich man with a quality and principle of life.

PARALLELISM

As noted above, much of the Wisdom literature is written in Hebrew poetry. Therefore, it is important that one understand a primary characteristic of Hebrew poetry—parallelism. Parallelism is defined as two or more lines of Hebrew poetry that are in some way related to each other. Furthermore, parallelism is divided into two parts—internal and external. Internal parallelism has to do with the smallest unit, usually two lines. External parallelism has to do with a large block of material, four or more lines.

An understanding of internal and external parallelism is very helpful in a study of the book of Proverbs. Very few individuals will desire to critically examine all the poetic sections of the Old Testament and analyze their parallel patterns, but the ability to pause periodically and examine a passage or two will greatly enhance one's study. It is with this thought in mind that we proceed to examine briefly parallelism in Wisdom Literature.

INTERNAL PARALLELISM

First, an examination of internal parallelism will be undertaken. There are basically six types of internal parallelism of interest to the student of Wisdom Literature:

(1) *Synonymous Internal Parallelism*—This parallelism is defined as two lines which say the same thing but in different words. An example of this is given in Psalms 24:1:

"The earth is the Lord's and the fulness thereof,
the world and those who dwell therein."

In this Psalm the first line states a truth and the second line clarifies the truth of the first line. In Psalm 24 "The earth" and "the world" are in parallel, and "the fulness" and "those who dwell" are in parallel and refer to the same thing, that is, "the people."

Another example of synonymous internal parallelism is Psalms 8:4:

"What is man that thou are mindful of him,
and the son of man that thou dost care for him?"

In this Psalm we note that "man" and "son of man" are in parallel, hence both refer to the same subject—man. From this it is evident that parallelism can be a great aid in helping the interpreter determine the meaning of some difficult words in a context. A good example of the value of parallelism is given in the KJV of Psalms 18:5:

"The sorrows of hell compassed me about:
the snares of death prevented me."

In this passage "hell" means simply "death" or "Sheol," the place of the dead, as in the RSV, and not the place of eternal torment. This, in turn, clears up a difficult passage in the KJV of Acts 2:27. In referring to Christ, the author of Acts 2:27 writes:

"Because thou wilt not leave my soul in hell,
neither will thou suffer thine Holy One to see corruption."

This passage in Acts simply means that Christ did not stay in the place of the dead, or death. The KJV of Matthew 16:18 is also clarified in this same manner.

(2) *Antithetic Internal Parallelism*—This parallelism is defined as poetry in which the second line teaches the same truth as the first line by making a contrast. An example of this is seen in Proverbs 15:1:

"A soft answer turns away wrath,
but a harsh word stirs up anger."

In this passage a soft word is contrasted with a hard, or harsh, word. The truth taught is the same but in contrast.

A second illustration of antithetic internal parallelism is Psalms 34:10:

"The young lions suffer want and hunger;
but those who seek the Lord lack no good thing."

Those who seek the Lord and their fate is contrasted with the young lions (probably a reference to the "unfaithful ones") and their fate. For two other illustrations of this parallelism see: Psalms 37:9 and Proverbs 14:28).

(3) *Synthetic or Formal Internal Parallelism*—This parallelism is defined as a situation in which the subject is stated and each succeeding line refers to the same subject but expands or enlarges it. In this type of parallelism each line makes a complete thought and it usually takes four lines to complete the intention of the writer in reference to the subject. For example, Psalms 121:3-8:

"He will not let your foot be moved, he who keeps you will not slumber.
Behold, he who keeps Israel will neither slumber nor sleep.
The Lord is your keeper; the Lord is your shade on your right hand.
The sun shall not smite you by day, nor the moon by night.
The Lord will keep you from all evil; he will keep your life.
The Lord will keep your going out and your coming in from this time forth and for evermore."

The key to this Psalm is the word "keep." The idea is that the Lord God keeps his people. Notice that each time the author speaks on the subject, "The Lord keeps his people," he enlarges his thought.

A second example of synthetic or formal internal parallelism is Psalms 19:7-9:

"The law of the Lord is perfect, reviving the soul;
the testimony of the Lord is sure, making wise the simple;
the precepts of the Lord are right, rejoicing the heart;
the commandment of the Lord is pure, enlightening the eyes;
the fear of the Lord is clean, enduring forever;
the ordinances of the Lord are true, and righteous altogether."

In this example each line describes God's Word with an adjective. This is followed with a second line which informs the reader what the Word of God does. For other examples of this type parallelism see: Psalms 14:1-2; 27:4; Job 17:1.

(4) *Emblematic Internal Parallelism*—This is a parallel arrangement in which a part is either a simile or a metaphor. A simile is a descriptive phrase using the words "like" or "as." A metaphor is a descriptive phrase which uses a word in an unusual way in order to suggest a likeness between ideas. It is distinguished from a simile by not employing any word of comparison such as "like" or "as." An example of this type parallelism is Psalms 103:11-13.

"For as the heavens are high above the earth,
so great is his steadfast love toward those who fear him;
as far as the east is from the west,
so far does he remove our transgressions from us.
As a father pities his children,
so the Lord pities those who fear him."

In Psalms 129:5-6 the author adopts this parallelism to reveal his hope that those who hate Zion will be overthrown as the grass on roof-tops:[4]

"May all who hate Zion be put to shame and turned backward!
Let them be like the grass on the housetops, which withers
    before it grows up."

(5) *Climatic or Stairlike Internal Parallelism*—Climatic parallelism is used to focus attention on the subject. In this type of parallelism, the second line usually repeats the first line and then proceeds on to complete the thought. For example, after reading verse 1a of Psalms 29 we ask, "Ascribe to the Lord what?" The second line answers this question, Psalms 29:1-2:

---

[4]It was common practice in Israel to plant flowers and grass on the roof-tops. Due to a lack of depth in soil, however, the vegetation would quickly die in the absence of moisture.

"Ascribe to the Lord, O heavenly beings,
ascribe to the Lord glory and strength.
Ascribe to the Lord the glory of his name;
worship the Lord in holy array."

This type of parallelism is called "stairlike" for it proceeds upward in thought like an individual walking up the stairwell. For example, Psalms 29:5a brings the question to our minds, "What cedars?" The second line, or next ascending line completes the thought, or answers the question: "The cedars of Labanon:

"The voice of the Lord breaks the cedars,
the Lord breaks the cedars of Lebanon."

For other examples of climatic internal parallelism the reader may refer to Psalms 92:9 and 96:7.

(6) *Inverted Internal Parallelism*—This type parallelism normally consists of four lines, but sometimes two lines, arranged in an a-b-b-a arrangement. A typical example of inverted internal parallelism is Isaiah 11:13b:

"Ephraim shall not be jealous of Judah,
and Judah shall not harass Ephraim."

This passage in Isaiah reads, "Ephraim . . . Judah; Judah . . . Ephraim." In the first line Ephraim is the subject and Judah is the direct object. In the second line this situation is reversed, or is an a-b-b-a arrangement.

Proverbs 23:15-16 is a second example of an a-b-b-a arrangement. In this passage line two is in parallel with line three, and line one is in parallel with line four:

"My son, if your heart is wise,
my heart too will be glad.
My soul⁵ will rejoice
when your lips speak what is right."

⁵The word "soul" in the Old Testament is the Hebrew word which is used most of the time to refer to the "whole man" or "the heart" of man.

EXTERNAL PARALLELISM

As was noted earlier, internal parallelism has to do with the smallest unit of Hebrew poetry, usually with two and sometimes four lines. External parallelism has to do with large blocks of Hebrew poetry, that is, four or more lines. For the purposes of this study, three types of external parallelism will be examined.

(1) *Synonymous External Parallelism*—This type parallelism has two lines of internal synonymous parallelism followed by two more lines of internal synonymous parallelism. It will be noted that both sets are synonymous, that is, teach the same truth. For example, Psalms 18:4-5:

> The cords of death encompassed me,
> the torrents of perdition assailed me;
> the cords of Sheol[6] entangled me,
> the snares of death confronted me.''

In this Psalm, "death," "perdition," and "Sheol" are synonymous, that is, all refer to the same place. A second illustration of synonymous external parallelism is Job 22:3-4:

> "Is it any pleasure to the Almighty if you are righteous,
> or is it gain to him if you make your ways blameless?
> Is it for your fear of him that he reproves you,
> and enters into judgment with you?''

(2) *Antithetic External Parallelism*—This parallelism is to be identified by two lines of internal synonymous parallelism followed by two lines of internal synonymous parallelism, but the second set of lines is not synonymous with the first set. This would be an a-b-c-d arrangement with a-b being synonymous and c-d being synonymous, but a-b will not be synonymous with c-d. Isaiah 1:3 is a typical example of this type parallelism:

> "The ox knows its owner,
> and the ass its master's crib;
> but Israel does not know,
> my people does not understand.''

---

[6]Here again, the KJV uses the word "hell" for the Hebrew "Sheol," which simply means the "place of the dead" and not eternal torment. The word used for the Hebrew "Sheol" in the LXX is "Hades," the "place of the dead."

In this passage the prophet laments the fact that the dumb animals know where to go to get nourishment, but Israel does not know where to turn in order to be spiritually nourished. The contrast is between dumb animals and the people of God.

(3) *Inverted External Parallelism*—This is always more than four lines and the lines are inverted in an a-b-c-c-b-a pattern. Isaiah 6:10 is such an arrangement using the words: heart-ears-eyes-eyes-ears-heart:

"Make the heart of this people fat,
and their ears heavy,
and shut their eyes;
lest they see with their eyes,
and hear with their ears,
and understand with their hearts,
and turn and be healed."

ACROSTIC AND RECURRING REFRAIN

There are two other basic types of Hebrew sentence arrangements used in Wisdom Literature which need to be mentioned at this time. These poetic arrangements are the acrostic and the recurring refrain:

(1) *Acrostic*—This is a composition in verse, or poem, in which each line, or set of lines begins with a succeeding letter of the alphabet. The Hebrew alphabet has twenty-two consonants, therefore, Hebrew acrostics will usually have twenty-two lines, or a multiple of twenty-two. For example, Proverbs 31:10-31 is an acrostic on the ideal woman. In this section of scripture, verse 10 begins with the Hebrew *alep* (A), verse 11 begins with the Hebrew *bet* (B), and so on down to the last verse which begins with the Hebrew *taw* (T).

Psalm 119 is also an acrostic. This acrostic contains eight lines which begin with the Hebrew *alep* (A), followed by eight lines which begin with the Hebrew *bet* (B), and so on through the Hebrew alphabet. With eight lines of each of the twenty-two Hebrew consonants, Psalm 119 concludes with 176 verses. Other Hebrew acrostics are found in Lamentations 1, 2, 4 and 5.

An early Christian acrostic familiar to many is the sign of the fish. The early century Christians took the Greek for "fish," *ICHTHUS,* and made the following acrostic:

I—*Iesous* = Jesus

CH—*Christos* = Christ

TH—*Theou* = of God

U—*Huios* = Son

S—*Soter* = Savior

(2) *Recurring Refrain*—This poetic arrangement is a series of verses followed by two or three lines of refrain, then, a new series of verses again followed by the same two or three lines of refrain, and so forth. An illustration of this type poetry is found in Psalms 42 and 43 which were probably one psalm originally. The reader will notice that the refrain is found at 42:5; 42:11 and 43:5 and is as follows:

"Why are you cast down, O my soul,
and why are you disquieted within me?
Hope in God, for I shall again praise him,
my help and my God."

It is easy to see the great value that acrostics and recurring refrains held for the Hebrew people. Such poetic arrangements were invaluable in aiding the people in their memorization of the Sacred Scriptures in the days before writing materials were easily accessible and affordable.

MAJOR EMPHASIS OF WISDOM LITERATURE

Wisdom literature is not primarily interested in history[7] and cult, for these were the interests of the prophets and priests. The exile was viewed as the failure of the cultic tradition, so Wisdom of post-exilic times especially took on a new interest, that of practical religion. The wise men were not greatly concerned with cultic life, and their references to the cult were frequently negative. This is not to say, however, that Wisdom was not interested in cultic traditions,

---

[7]Some might take exception to this idea and note a priestly concern in Wisdom's emphasis on creation, universalism, and the transcendence of God. See: Glenden E. Bryce, "Omen-Wisdom in Ancient Israel," *Journal of Biblical Literature,* Volume 94, Number 1 (March, 1975), 19-37.

for such was involved in the "fear of Yahweh" so stressed by the wise men. In contrast to the cultic emphasis of the prophet and priest, Wisdom emphasized the importance of practical, every day living in righteousness. It speaks of nature, family, social relations, common occupations, etc. Righteousness entails common sense moral intelligence judgments more than a dependence on God laying out righteousness in a cultic situation.

Wisdom literature was also theocentric. The major difference between the Wisdom of Israel and its pagan neighbors is that Israel's Wisdom placed wickedness and righteousness alongside the moral teachings and character of its God. Wisdom also differed from the cultic traditions of God within its own nation, that is, Wisdom brought God out of the realm of the cultic experience and put him into the realm of the Creator of all things, no matter how minute and insignificant.

The major emphasis of Wisdom, therefore, is to set forth a practical and teachable moral way of life in relation to the God of Israel. Wisdom is a practical way of life governed by practical advice. By studying and applying such advice, an individual can be taught to be wise.

Introduction to the
Text of Proverbs

TITLE

The book of Proverbs takes its name from the opening words of the text, "The Proverbs of Solomon, son of David, king of Israel" (Proverbs 1:1). The designation known to the Jews for this work was *mishele,* from *mashal,* a concise saying which expresses religious or worldly wisdom and ethics. In the Septuagint the title is *Paroimiae Salomontos* ("proverbs of Solomon"), and in the Latin Vulgate, Jerome entitled the book *Liber Proverbiorum* ("the Book of Proverbs"). Many of the early Christians referred to this book as *Sophia* ("Wisdom").

TYPES OF PROVERBS

The word "proverb" *(mishele)* means "to be like, a comparison; noting likeness in things unlike." A *mishele* is the most common type of proverb, being a brief saying of popular sagacity making a point on practical experience. Hanneberg[1] has divided some of the various types of proverbs as follows:

(1) **Historical**—This is a popular proverbial saying which expresses a general truth or idea based on a historical event, or some other consequential circumstance. An example of a historical proverb is 1 Samuel 10:12: "And a man of the place answered, 'And who is their father?' Therefore it became a proverb, 'Is Saul also among the prophets?' " This proverb corresponds roughly to our proverbial phrase, "A fish out of water." The presence of Saul in a prophetic circle was no doubt surprising to the onlookers. He was a man of

---

[1]Taken from W. J. Deane and S. T. Taylor-Taswell, *The Pulpit Commentary,* Volume 9. Proverbs, (Grand Rapids, 1962), p iii. Used by permission of the publisher, Eerdmans Publishing Co.

great ability, but certainly not the type one might expect to find among the prophets.

A second illustration of a historical proverb is Ezekiel 18:2: "The fathers have eaten sour grapes, and the children's teeth are set on edge." This was a popular saying among the Jews of Ezekiel's day, and its interpretation was that the people of God in Babylonian exile blamed their fathers for their troubles. This proverb was partly true, but it did not justify the sins of the present generation. The Lord God took this popular saying and negated it by stating, "The soul that sins shall die" (Ezekiel 18:4b). The Israelites could no longer blame their sins on anyone but themselves.

A modern day illustration of a historical proverb may be the American classic, "Remember the Alamo." There seem to be no historical proverbs in the book of Proverbs.

(2) **Metaphorical**—These proverbs use a figure of speech in which a name, action, or descriptive term characteristic of one object from nature or life is applied to another to suggest a likeness between them. Here we have the idea (like) that expressed with the biblical "Like people, like priest" (Hosea 4:9). In this proverb, Hosea reveals that the priests and people will stand alike in the judgment of God. This same figure of likeness is expressed in Ezekiel's "Like mother, like daughter" (Ezekiel 16:44), a taunting proverb comparing the apostate Jerusalem with the Canaanites. Jerusalem has so adopted the Canaanite ways that she had become like a daughter imitating her mother, the Canaanite. See also: Proverbs 19:13; 27:15-16 for other metaphorical proverbs dealing with humanity.

Metaphorical proverbs also have to do with the area of nature, as in Proverbs 1:17: "For in vain is a net spread in the sight of any bird." This appears to mean that as clear as the warning is to the birds, it is vain, for they still fly into the net and are entrapped. The lesson is that the great net of God's judgment is spread out, open to the eyes of all, yet the wicked still rush into it. Likewise, in Proverbs 17:12: "Let a man meet a she-bear robbed of her cubs, rather than a fool[2] in his folly." What greater type of savagery could there be than a large brown bear of Syria robbed of her cubs? (*cf.* 2 Samuel 17:8; 2 Kings 2:24. See also: Proverbs 6:6.)

---

[2]A "fool" *(kesil)* is one who hates knowledge (Proverbs 1:22), delights not in understanding (Proverbs 18:2), and delights in mischief (Proverbs 10:23). A fool has no desire to do right in the sight of God.

(3) **Riddle**—The best illustration of a riddle-type proverb is that of Samson's in Judges 14:14: "And he said to them, 'Out of the eater came something to eat. Out of the strong came something sweet.' And they could not in three days tell what the riddle was." Oriental literature is full of such obscure, enigmatic language which is unriddled by some clever person. Daniel was noted for his skill in resolving such riddles (Daniel 5:12). The riddle of Samson's was not solved by the men of Timnah until they worked through his wife to get the answer. When Samson discovered this he again replied in a riddle: "If you had not plowed with my heifer, you would not have found out my riddle" (Judges 14:18), that is, if the men of Timnah had not worked through Samson's wife to get the answer to the riddle, they would never have known it.

A second example of a riddle-type proverb is Proverbs 30:4:

> "Who has ascended to heaven and come down?
> Who has gathered the wind in his fists?
> Who has wrapped up the waters in a garment?
> Who has established all the ends of the earth?
> What is his name, and what is his son's name?
> Surely you know!"

This riddle reveals the ignorance of man and his nothingness as compared with the wisdom and power of God. It also reveals that such proverbs (as riddles) set forth questions which need deep thought to solve and which convey moral truths. See also: Proverbs 30:11-31.

(4) **Allegorical**—This is an extended metaphor, or simile, used by the people of biblical times for presenting truths. Usually such allegories, or parables, became brief narratives such as Ezekiel 17:2-10. From this passage in Ezekiel, one can understand that this type proverb explains its ethical object by a resemblance from the region of nature and every day life. Proverbs 9:1 is another example of the allegorical proverb: "Wisdom has built her house, she has set up seven pillars." An analysis of Jesus' teaching indicates that this was a favorite method of his.

(5) **Didactical**—This type of proverb reveals the primary intention of the book of Proverbs, that is, to be a source book of materials for instructing in morals, religion and behavior. Didactical proverbs deal with all phases of human life and behavior, as well as man's relation to God. The first nine chapters of Proverbs reveal such didactical emphasis.

OBJECT OF PROVERBS

The book of Proverbs is not, of course, simply a collection of choice literary extracts of moral and religious sayings commonly heard in ancient Israel. It is a source book of instructional materials for teaching Jewish youth in a school and the more mature individual and simply to be used for private study. Its object is to cultivate personal morality and practical wisdom, to regulate life in all its conditions in order to achieve the good life. This object is set forth at the very beginning of the book:

"That men may know wisdom and instruction, understand words of insight, receive instruction in wise dealing, righteousness, justice, and equity; that prudence may be given to the simple, knowledge and discretion to the youth— the wise man also may hear and increase in learning, and the man of understanding acquire skill" (Proverbs 1:2-5)

Proverbs is partly moral and partly intellectual. It is founded upon human experience in relation to God and community life, and it seeks to instruct the young in the way of wisdom, to edify those who have already made progress, and to discipline all to receive and assimilate the highest teachings. In other words, Proverbs is concerned with the practical religion necessary to deal with the conduct of life. It teaches duty to God, to oneself and to neighbors, as well as domestic duties and civil and political responsibilites.

AUTHORSHIP OF PROVERBS

Most Jewish commentators and many of the early Christian Church fathers ascribe the complete book of Proverbs to one author, Solomon, king of Israel. This view was adopted by the early Church fathers because of the absence or obscurity of the titles of Proverbs 30 and 31 in the Greek and Latin manuscripts. Solomonic authorship was also motivated by 1 Kings 4:32, which reads that Solomon "uttered three thousand proverbs; and his songs were a thousand and five." This number certainly exceeds the number preserved in our present-day book of Proverbs, which contains about eight hundred lines. This, accompanied by the claim that Solomon's "wisdom surpassed the wisdom of all the people of the east, and all the wisdom of Egypt" (1 Kings 4:30), was why Solomon's name became attached to this piece of Wisdom literature.

It must be noted, however, that three portions of the book are ascribed to Solomon: Proverbs 1:1; 10:1 and 25:1. Surely these subtitles would have been unnecessary if the preceding material in each case, and indeed the whole book, were from Solomon. Two sections are attributed to other writers; one to Agur (Proverbs 30:1), and the other to Lemuel (Proverbs 31:1). There are also two appendices (Proverbs 22:17; 24:23) which attribute these writings to "the words of the wise." It seems, therefore, that the book of Proverbs is the result of at least three writers, Solomon, Agur, and Lemuel.

Those who hold to the Solomonic authorship have an explanation for Agur and Lemuel, however. Such interpreters state that Agur (Hebrew: *Agur*) means "gatherer" or "collector" and is a symbolic name for Solomon who was noted as a collector or gatherer of wisdom and maxims. By the same token, Lemuel (Hebrew: *Limuel*) means "God-ward" or "unto God," the equivalent of "dedicated to God," and also refers to Solomon. Solomon was, from infancy, dedicated to God, and was, in fact, called by God, "Jedidiah," beloved of the Lord (2 Samuel 12:25).

The most probable view, after examining the evidence, is that Proverbs is a collection of maxims by many authors. The title (Proverbs 1:1) cannot be taken as a guarantee that all of the book is the sole work of Solomon. The reasons for this are as follows:[3]

(1) The contents and language point to differences of date and composition. It appears that the book contains at least the language of Solomon's time,[4] the language of a later post-exilic editor,[5] and the writings of other wise men, particularly Agur and Lemuel, whose times we know nothing of.

(2) The repetition of the same proverbs in identical, or almost identical, language. For example, compare Proverbs 14:12 with 16:25; Proverbs 25:24 with 21:9; Proverbs 26:22 with 18:8.

(3) The recurrence of the same thoughts varied only in actual wording. For example, compare Proverbs 10:1 with 15:20; Proverbs 14:20 with 19:4.

---

[3]Deane and Taylor-Taswell, *op cit, p xvi.*
[4]Many words and grammatical pecularities in Proverbs point to strong Ugaritic and Phoenician influence and Phoenician origin. This points to pre-exilic times.
[5]Parts of the book reveal a highly developed essay style such as in Hellenistic literature, as well as Aramaisms. The way in which "wisdom" and "folly" are personified also seems to betray Hellenistic influence.

(4) Variations in the language, which in a very marked manner differentiate the several parts, so that one is forced to allow a composite character to the work.

(5) The reference to the law and prophecy (vision) in Proverbs 29:18 and 30:5-6, tend to support a date after the time of Ezra.

Thus, while tradition ascribes the book of Proverbs to Solomon, we must realize that it was, no doubt, Solomon's patronship, not authorship, that is meant when the work is attributed to him. Solomon's name came to be associated with Proverbs by literary convention, although the material came from many unidentifiable sources. Proverbs would, therefore, be parallel in its composition to Psalms. It is a collection of the sayings of the wise men of Israel, taking its name from the chief wise man, Solomon, just as the Psalms are a collection of hymns from many sources,[6] but attributed to the chief hymn-writer, David.

DATE OF PROVERBS

In only one place can we ascertain with any certainty the date of any portion of the book of Proverbs. According to Proverbs 25:1, a section of this work was copied by the men of Hezekiah from previous records: "These also are proverbs of Solomon which the men of Hezekiah king of Judah copied." These proverbs were compiled during the reign of Hezekiah between two and three hundred years after the time of Solomon. That Hezekiah has a reign of literary activity is evident from such passages as 2 Kings 18:18, 37 and 19:2-3 (cf. Isaiah 38:10-20). Hezekiah's literary activity was so great that Jewish tradition stated: "Hezekiah and his company wrote the Proverbs" (*Baba Bathra* 15a). This reference was probably speaking of the editorship of the book of Proverbs and not the actual writing of proverbs.

W. F. Albright contends that the book of Proverbs in "its entire content"[7] is probably pre-exilic, but that much of it was orally transmitted until the fifth century B.C. In contrast to this view, Eissfeldt holds that the book is post-exilic, no earlier than the fourth century B.C.[8] Eissfeldt supports his argument by stating that Proverbs betrays Grecian influence and Aramaic words.

---

[6]Such as the sons of Korah (Psalms 47).

[7]H. H. Rowley, *Wisdom in Israel and the Ancient Near East* (Highlands, N.J., 1960), p 13.

[8]O. Eissfeldt, *Kleine Schriften,* I and II.

The final compilation of the book of Proverbs appears to be post-exilic and dates around the year 400 B.C., although the bulk of the work is pre-exilic. As pointed out by Eissfeldt, the Aramaisms seem to point to the collection and re-editing process carried out by later compilers. According to Blank, "Proverbs was certainly complete with title page before the time of Ben Sirach (ca 190 B.C.) who alludes in 47:17 to Proverbs 1:6, and who develops further certain thoughts and trends evident in Proverbs."[9]

CHARACTERISTICS AND TEACHINGS OF PROVERBS

(1) *Universalism*—This characteristic of Proverbs reflects the foreign origin of much of Israel's Wisdom literature. Proverbs is concerned with man in general and not just the nation of Israel. In fact, the name "Israel" is not mentioned at all in Proverbs. The Lord God is viewed as Creator, and as such, is the Father of all nations. Therefore, the behavior standards set forth in Proverbs by the Hebrew wise men reflect the laws of this Creator, and therefore, are to be the standards for every culture. Thus, the morality set forth in Proverbs is not just the result of the observation of good and evil in various cultures, on the contrary, it is a morality grounded in the precepts given Israel by her God. In fact, the fear of the Lord stood as the very foundation of Wisdom: "The fear of the Lord is the beginning of knowledge" (Proverbs 1:7). In commenting on this universal approach, Delitzsch wrote that the wise man utilizes the truthfulness of God's revelation to Israel and then moves to "comprehend those general ideas in which could already be discovered the fitness of the religion of *Jahve* for becoming the world-religion."[10]

(2) *Simplicity*—There is a tendency in Proverbs to over-emphasize the simplicity in the character of human nature. There are three basic classes of men listed in the book:

(i) The wise, or righteous (Proverbs 10:1-3). These individuals are ones whose life-styles are characterized by high ethical qualities and attitudes of fear, or reverence, toward God.

---

[9]S. H. Blank, "Proverbs, Book of," *The Interpreter's Dictionary of the Bible*, 1962, Volume 3, 940.

[10]F. Delitzsch, *Keil-Delitzsch Commentary on the Old Testament*, Volume VI, *Proverbs, Ecclesiastes, Song of Solomon*, (Grand Rapids, 1973), p 41. Used by permission of the publisher, Eerdmans Publishing Co.

(ii) The simple (Proverbs 9:4). These individuals are ones who are mislead by their foolishness, or simple-mindedness. There is great hope for such individuals, however, for they may be reclaimed through discipline (Proverbs 19:25; 21:11).

(iii) The fools, or wicked (Proverbs 10:1-3). The "fool" is the man who, whether from weakness of character, or from stubbornness, lacks the perception necessary to guide him in the paths of righteousness. He is distinguished from the "simple" by the fact that he is self-sufficient in spiritual and intellectual matters.

(3) *Practical*—Proverbs is not spiritually centered for its main concern is how to become wise and not be foolish. The wise men assumed the main postulates of Israel's religion and applied themselves to establishing morality upon the basis of principles common to humanity at large. This is a book teaching a course in applied religion, taken from the world of human affairs as well as the world of nature also. To be wise, one must develop positive attitudes: patience, generosity, modesty, trustworthiness, benevolence to the poor, etc. To become wise, one must also avoid certain pitfalls such as laziness (Proverbs 23:29-35), drunkenness (Proverbs 5:1-6), and loose women (Proverbs 5:1-6).

(4) *Strict View of Retribution*—There is immediate material success as the reward for a good life and failure for the wicked life emphasized in Proverbs. Health, wealth, honor and long life are to be seen as visible evidence of divine approval: "The reward for humility and fear of the Lord is riches and honor and life. Thorns and snares are in the way of the perverse" (Proverbs 22:4-5a). The principle that men are rewarded in this life according to their works, pervades the entire book. The wise and the foolish, their different aims and situations in life, are contrasted with great frequency.

The reader is impressed with the high ethical standards set forth in Proverbs, yet, in spite of this, goodness is almost always motivated by personal interest or success. For example: "Do not rejoice when your enemy falls, and let not your heart be glad when he stumbles; lest the Lord see it, and be displeased, and turn away his anger from him" (Proverbs 24:17-18. See also Proverbs 25:21-22). He who is wise will conduct himself in such a way that he will live a long, happy and prosperous life. The good man receives his rewards of happiness, prosperity and long life here on earth; the wicked man is punished by a premature or violent death.

(5) *Conservatism*—This reflects an upper class life and concern for

the stability of the society's institutions. Wisdom manifests itself in living according to the moral norms of the covenant community. The family life is placed on a high pedestal of morality as is also respect for the government officials and the community government.

(6) *Piety*—Proverbs has religious interests. Attention to all matters in everyday life is of little consequence if one does not fear God. The attribute of God as Creator occurs many times in Proverbs. There is little reference to Hebrew history, salvation-history, religious tradition, etc. The book completely ignores the obligations of temple worship and cultic festivals, which occupy so prominent a place in the religious consciousness of Israel. Wisdom is viewed as a personified agent of God (Proverbs 3:19-20; 8:22-31), and although not theological in nature, Wisdom is concerned with fear of God. It will also be noted that Israel's Wisdom theologizes the Wisdom literature of other nations.

In conclusion, we can say that the theology of Proverbs reaffirms the place of everyday life in God's complete plan and purpose. The book of Proverbs stresses individual morality; it has a regard for community life; and it emphasizes the doctrine of retributive justice. While the book appears to have little to say concerning the temple and cultic festivals, as well as the Law and its commandments, we must realize that the priest, prophet and the wise man work together in the life of a nation of God's people. The total result of all these teachers makes up the religious life of the people of God.

Commentary on Proverbs

THE STRUCTURE OF THIS STUDY

That Proverbs is a part of the Old Testament canon verifies the fact that Wisdom literature is included in the revelation of God's plan for the life of his people. Proverbs is not merely the accumulation of many intelligent observations on life either. Rather it is an inspired book of instructions deemed important in man's education, both the inexperienced and the wise. Jesus Christ linked himself with the Wisdom of the Old Testament when he said: "The queen of the South will arise at the judgment with the men of this generation and condemn them; for she came from the ends of the earth to hear the wisdom of Solomon, and behold, something greater than Solomon is here" (Luke 11:31; cf. Matthew 12:42). This word from Jesus Christ seems to imply that the Wisdom of the Old Testament, so imperfectly revealed in the character and teachings of Solomon, is now perfectly and powerfully manifested in the lifestyle and teachings of Jesus.

In this study of the book of Proverbs, we will divide the book into four major sections: Wisdom—God—Man—Numerical Riddles, rather than study it on a chapter-by-chapter division. Prior to examining what Proverbs reveals about these four areas, however, it will be necessary to define Wisdom, and in defining it, view it from a negative point, that is, what Wisdom is not, and from a positive point of view, what Wisdom is.

The inspired writer informs us that "The fear of the Lord is the beginning of knowledge; fools despise wisdom and instruction" (Proverbs 1:7). From a knowledge of Hebrew internal synonymous parallelism, we determine that Wisdom is defined as "the fear of the Lord." So, a wise man is a man of wisdom, or a fearer of the Lord. This, then, brings up the question, "What is the fear of the Lord?, or wisdom?

THE FEAR OF THE LORD

Approaching the study of Wisdom, or fear of the Lord, from the negative point of view, we will first note that the fear of the Lord is not:

(1) The Wicked Man's Fear—According to Isaiah 57:20-21, "The wicked are like the tossing sea; for it cannot rest, and its waters toss up mire and dirt. There is no peace, says my God, for the wicked." In contrast to this life-style, Jesus promised: "Come to me, all who labor and are heavy laden, and I will give you rest. Take my yoke upon you, and learn from me, for I am gentle and lowly in heart, and you will find rest for your souls. For my yoke is easy, and my burden is light" (Matthew 11:28-30). The wicked are agitated like troubled waters, ever tossing in the misery of sin, bringing forth the thoughts, works and words of an evil conscience, as the turbulent sea brings up the mire and dirt from its bottom. In contrast, those who fear the Lord have the peace of mind and heart that comes from knowing the care and concern of God, the Father. Thus, fear of the Lord is not the same thing as the wicked man's fear.

(2) The Fear of Calamity—In the days of King Ahaz of Judah, the people of God had a great fear of attack from Syria and Ephraim (Isaiah 7:1—9:1). Samaria (or Ephraim) and Syria had leagued themselves against Ahaz of Judah. At this time, the Lord God sent Isaiah to assure Ahaz that he should not fear these two nations, but that he should trust in God. In spite of God's urging, however, Ahaz went to Assyria for help. The result of this disobedience to God brought no peace to Ahaz and his people; on the contrary, it brought fear. God, however, assured Isaiah, "Do not call conspiracy all that this people call conspiracy, and do not fear what they fear nor be in dread. But the Lord of hosts, him you shall regard as holy; let him be your fear, and let him be your dread" (Isaiah 8:12-13). The disobedient Judeans had a great fear of calamity, but faithful Isaiah feared only the Lord God. Therefore, the fear of the Lord is different from a fear of calamity.

The apostle Peter points out this same truth, that is, the fear of the Lord is not the same as the fear of calamity: "Now who is there to harm you if you are zealous for what is right? But even if you do suffer for righteousness' sake, you will be blessed. Have no fear of them, nor be troubled, but in your hearts reverence[1] Christ as Lord" (1 Peter 3:13-15). Peter is quoting from the LXX (Greek translation of the Old Testament) of Isaiah 8:12-13, and urges Christians to fear the Lord, not persecution, affliction, or sufferings. So, again, fear of the Lord is not the same thing as the fear of calamity. The Lord is to "be our fear and dread" (Isaiah 8:13).

(3) The Fearful Expectation of Judgment—The writer of Hebrews informs his readers that they can expect a fearful prospect of judgment only when they sin willfully: "For if we sin deliberately after receiving a knowledge of the truth, there no longer remains a sacrifice for sins, but a fearful prospect of judgment, and a fury of fire which will consume the adversaries" (Hebrews 10:26-27). To live in deliberate sin is to reject the mercy and love of God. It is to turn from the God of mercy and encounter the God of wrath. Such a life-style of rejecting God results in a certain fearful anticipation of the coming judgment.

In contrast to this fear of the wicked on the day of judgment are the promises to the faithful: "He (God) will render to every man according to his works: to those who by patience in well-doing seek for glory and honor and immorality, he will give eternal life. . . . There will be . . . glory and honor and peace for every one who does good, the Jew first and also the Greek" (Romans 2:6-7, 9-10). The apostle John wrote that "we may have confidence for the day of judgment" (1 John 4:17); and Jude assures Christians that Christ "is able to keep you from falling and to present you without blemish before the presence of his glory with rejoicing" (Jude 24).

From this we can be assured that the fear of the Lord has reached its true end, or purpose in our lives—it has come to its desired end and development—when we have full confidence in the Lord. The result of such fear is confidence on the day of judgment. This confidence is a supreme instance of the full realization of the divine love in our midst. There can be no fear of judgment for those who know themselves to be endowed with the proper fear of the Lord, therefore, fear of the Lord is not the fearful expectation of judgment.

---

[1]As we will learn later, "reverence" means the same thing as "to fear" in this context.

Viewing the subject "the fear of the Lord" from a negative standpoint, it was noted that the fear of the Lord is not the same thing as the wicked man's fear, the fear of calamity, or the fearful expectation of judgment. What, then, is the fear of the Lord? The answer to this question will be evident after examination of several passages of scripture, in both the Old and New Testaments, that pertain to this subject. From a positive viewpoint, the fear of the Lord is:

(1) To Stand in Awe of the Lord—In Malachi 2:5b we have an example of Hebrew internal synonymous parallelism: "And he feared me, he stood in awe of my name." In this passage, "feared" is synonymous with "awe," and "me" is synonyous with "my name." Therefore, to fear the Lord is to stand in awe of him. God's promised life and peace to the priests would become a reality if they would be true and faithful to the covenant. The response of the priests should have been one of reverence and awe. When the priests responded in this manner to God, the covenant stood firm and God and the priesthood were in harmony.

A second example of this fear of the Lord, or awe, is found in Malachi 1:6: "A son honors his father, and a servant his master. If then I am a father, where is my honor? And if I am a master, where is my fear? says the Lord of hosts . . .". A child of God, then, is to fear the Lord like a servant fears his master. If God is Lord and Master, there is to be honor and respect due him from his servants.

Another illustration of this fear, or awe, is found in Job 1:8: "And the Lord said to Satan, 'Have you considered my servant Job, that there is none like him on the earth, a blameless and upright man, who fears God and turns away from evil?' " Now, this fear was not a fear of wrath, but of honor, respect, etc. The servant in ancient times was considered a part of his master's household and could even inherit the family's goods, if there were no sons. A case in point is the situation that existed with Abraham and Eliezer of Damascus (Genesis 15:1-2). From this we note that fear of the Lord is not a fearful, trembling emotion, but rather a standing in awe of the Lord as in a servant-master relationship.

(2) To Respect or Reverence the Lord—To fear the Lord entails fearing God like a citizen fears the king. In Joshua 4:14 (KJV) we read: "On that day the Lord magnified Joshua in the sight of all Israel; and they feared him as they feared Moses, all the days of his life." This "fear" of Joshua on the part of the people motivated

them to place great confidence in the leadership of this man of God. To fear the Lord, therefore, involves placing confidence in him as being fully able to guide and protect his followers.

A second illustration of this fear is found in 1 Kings 3:28: "And all Israel heard of the judgment which the king had judged; and they feared the king, for they saw that the wisdom of God was in him to do judgment." This passage concerned the judgment of Solomon's involving the two women living in the same house and their dispute as to whose child was dead and whose was alive. Solomon's almost supernatural wisdom in deciding the maternity of the child by offering to cut it in two resulted in "fear" or "awe" (RSV) on the part of the women as well as all Israel.

In the New Testament, Paul admonishes Christians: "Pay all of them their dues, . . . respect ("fear," *phobon,* KJV) to whom respect is due, honor to whom honor is due" (Romans 13:7). The apostle Paul exhorts the brethren to exercise respect and subjection to their rulers, as well as veneration that belongs to them as ministers of God. Therefore, the fear of the Lord entails similar respect and veneration like that given to a leader of the people, with the exception that such respect of the Lord must be infinitely higher.

(3) To Honor the Lord—A person is to honor the Lord God as a child honors his parents. In Leviticus 19:3 we read that each child "shall revere ("fear," KJV) his mother and his father." In the New Testament, Hebrews 12:9 states that "we have had earthly fathers to discipline us and we respected them. Shall we not much more be subject to the Father of spirits and live?" As the family life can only function well and in harmony with such parental respect, so too, the family of God can only function in righteousness when each member of that family has the proper reverence and obedience in his relationship with God. Such respect is forthcoming from God's people when they understand that God always acts in a way that is beneficial to the ones who fear him. This fact is vividly illustrated in internal emblematic parallelism in Psalms 103:13:

"As a father pities his children,
so the Lord pities those who fear him."

The fear that belongs to the Lord God is also expressed in Psalms 111:9b as two adjectives are given to describe God: "Holy and terrible is his name." The word "terrible" entails the idea that God's name, or person, elicits fear or awe from man. In ancient thought a name was supposed to gather up and express the attributes of a person, hence, God's attributes are such that he is to be reverenced.

(4) To Regard the Lord—A person is to fear or regard the Lord God. An illustration of what it means to "regard" the Lord is given in the book of Exodus in relation to God's actions against Pharoah: "Then he who feared the word of the Lord among the servants of Pharaoh made his slaves and his cattle flee into the houses; but he who did not regard the word of the Lord left his slaves and his cattle in the field" (Exodus 9:20-21). The Hebrew word for "regard" is literally "to set the heart" *(sum leb)*. So, to regard the Lord is to "set the heart" to believe in the power and truthfulness of him.

In the New Testament this word "regard" is expressed by Luke as he relates a parable of Jesus: "In a certain city there was a judge who neither feared God nor regarded man . . ." (Luke 18:2). Here, "regard" reveals a lack of concern or interest in the things pertaining to God or man (*cf* Matthew 21:37). Such an individual is controlled by his own ideas and inclinations and not by any sense of a higher power or justice. In contrast to this lack of "regard" is Jesus who "was heard for his godly fear" (Hebrews 5:7).

(5) To Fear the Lord As A Wife Fears Her Husband—Man is to fear the Lord God like a godly wife fears her husband. Paul writes: "Let the wife see that she respects ("reverence," KJV) her husband" (Ephesians 5:33). The apostle Peter also comments on this relationship: "Likewise your wives, be submissive to your husbands, so that some, though they do not obey the word, may be won without a word by the behavior of their wives, when they see your reverent and chaste behavior" (1 Peter 3:1-2). Peter goes on to point out that "Sarah obeyed Abraham, calling him Lord" (1 Peter 3:6a). This "fear" entails not only love, but respect and obedience. It is the rejection of the desire for autonomy, self-sufficiency and self-domination. To fear the Lord is to recognize his headship, or lordship, as the controlling authority deserving of obedience.

By way of summation, we present these points as to what fear of the Lord involves:

Fear of the Lord is:	Fear of the Lord is like:
(1) To stand in awe of	(1) The slave-master relationship
(2) To respect or reverence	(2) The citizen-king relationship
(3) To honor	(3) The child-parent relationship
(4) To regard	(4) The Jesus-God relationship
	(5) The wife-husband relationship

Up to this point in our study we have examined what "fear of the Lord" is and to what it can be compared in one's everyday relationships. In an attempt to show the importance and relevance of this fear in our lives, we now concern ourselves with the question, "What does 'fear of the Lord' lead an individual to do?" Fear of the Lord leads a person to:

(1) Work Righteousness—In his sermon to Cornelius, the apostle Peter said: "Truly I perceive that God shows no partiality, but in every nation any one who fears him and does what is right ("worketh righteousness"—KJV) is acceptable to him" (Acts 10:34-35). In this passage, fearing God is equated with working righteousness, and such places an individual in a state preparatory to the salvation received through Christ. With the fear of God as the controlling motive in one's life, the individual is led to a life-style of continual awareness of God's presence. Such awareness will greatly influence one's disposition and attitude toward God and man.

(2) Keep God's Commandments—"The fear of the Lord is the beginning of wisdom; a good understanding have all they that do his commandments" (Psalms 111:10, KJV). The writer of Ecclesiastes adds his voice to this matter with these words: "The end of the matter; all has been heard. Fear God, and keep his commandments; for this is the whole duty of man" (Ecclesiastes 12:13). As we have seen earlier, the "fear of the Lord" means "reverence for the Lord," and is a comprehensive term for the worship, ritual and morality of the people of God. Such a life of reverence comes as a result of keeping God's commandments. A genuine "fear of the Lord" is synonymous with a genuine heartfelt service to him. Fear, as a prominent emotion in our spiritual life, is not, therefore, the terror of a slave, who would willingly, if he could, break away from his owner, but the loving reverence of a child who is anxious to avoid anything that would grieve his father's heart. Such fear, resulting in a love for the heavenly Father, leads one to keep God's commandments.

(3) Serve God—In Joshua 24 the successor of Moses, Joshua, stood before the people of God at Shechem as they took upon themselves a covenant with the Lord God. At this time, Joshua spoke: "Now therefore fear the Lord, and serve him in sincerity and in faithfulness" (Joshua 24:14a). Joshua was calling upon the people of Israel to rely completely on the promises given them by God in this covenant. In our age, fear of the Lord will cause us, in a

free and moral way, to serve the Lord and him alone.

(4) Depart from Evil—Several passages in the Bible reveal this aspect of a proper fear of the Lord. In speaking to Satan concerning Job, the Lord God said: "There is none like him on the earth, a blameless and upright man, who fears God and turns away from evil" (Job 1:8; cf Job 2:3). Job is a blameless, or mature, individual, an ace of a man, who feared the Lord. This fear of the Lord manifested by Job gave God confidence in the patriarch's ability to overcome the assaults of Satan.

In Job 28:28 we read, again, the definition of "fear of the Lord": "Behold, the fear of the Lord, that is wisdom; and to depart from evil is understanding" (cf Proverbs 3:7; 8:13; 14:16; 16:16). "Fear of the Lord" is a practical attitude of human behavior which entails obedience and the avoidance of evil. Fear of the Lord, therefore, stands in very close relationship with one's manner of life, that is, fear, or reverence for God, leads one to avoid conduct out of harmony with his covenant relationship with his heavenly Father.

By way of summary, "fear of the Lord" will lead an individual to do the following:

(1) Work righteousness   (3) Serve God
(2) Keep God's commandments   (4) Depart from evil

WISDOM

With the definition of "wisdom" or "fear of the Lord" behind us, we now proceed into a study to determine what the book of Proverbs has to say about wisdom. In this study we will note that the primary aim of the book is centered around the relationship of wisdom to one's religion. It is only the wise man that can possibly be the man that stands in a right relationship with God. What, then, does the book of Proverbs inform us about wisdom?

(1) The Aim of the Book of Proverbs—Even a casual reading of Proverbs 1:2-7 reveals that the object, or purpose, of the book is to instruct the inexperienced (verse 4) in the way of wisdom, and to further instruct the more mature (verse 5). Again, we note that wisdom is more than mental knowledge and learning. It is a knowing coupled with doing. Jesus taught this identical principle: "Every one then who hears these words of mine and does them will be like a wise man who built his house upon the rock" (Matthew 7:24). Wisdom, or "fear of the Lord," is, then, the expression of that

knowledge of God as revealed in one's conduct toward God and man. It is the purpose of Proverbs to elicit such a way of life from both the mature and the immature in the faith.

The reference in Proverbs 1:4 to "the youth" has led many to believe that this advice is given to young men just entering government service to the royal family. This might have been the original intent of Proverbs, but certainly the broader objective of intellectual and moral training of young men for life in the Jewish community must have been included in its purpose also. When this aim of Proverbs is accomplished in the lives of the recipients of wisdom, then the life of the community will be greatly enriched.

The word "simple" in Proverbs 1:4 does not mean a simpleton, but is rather from the Hebrew word *pethaim* (from the verb *pethach*—"to open"), and refers to one is open about any outside influence. This word "simple" is in parallel with "youth" and so expresses the idea of immaturity and inexperience. Again, Proverbs is to be used to give knowledge and discretion,[2] or the ability to plan and gain the right and desired end in one's life.

Not only are the young to benefit from the wisdom teaching in the book of Proverbs, however, for even those who are wise and with understanding can gain in learning and skill (*cf* Proverbs 1:5). Proverbs has a message of wisdom for all classes of people. From this we realize that wisdom, or "fear of the Lord," is not something which stops with the passing of the years of youth. The wise man may even "acquire skill," or literally, "acquire the power to rightly steer his course" (Proverbs 1:5b). This idea parallels Paul's thought to the Corinthian Christians: "Yet among the mature we do impart wisdom . . ." (1 Corinthians 2:6). One of the great traits of the Word of God is that it imparts wisdom to all levels of intelligence and understanding. No one is ever of such understanding that he or she cannot be informed and instructed by God's Word. No matter how wise, or "mature," a man may be, there is still room within every character to grow in the wisdom of God.

Proverbs 1:7 can be viewed as the theme of the book. "The fear of the Lord is the beginning of knowledge." "Beginning" (Hebrew—*reshith*) carries with it the idea of "starting point," as in Genesis 1:1: "In the beginning God created the heavens and the earth." It means also the "chief" or "choice" part as in Jeremiah

---

[2]Discretion as used here entails the meaning of the power to decide one's own course in life.

49:35: "Thus saith the Lord of hosts; Behold, I will break the bow of Elam, the chief of their might" (KJV; cf Amos 6:6, KJV). The "fear of the Lord" is, therefore, not only the starting point of all true knowledge, but the primary thing, or the chief part of one's knowledge and wisdom (cf Proverbs 9:10; Job 28:28; Psalms 111:10; Ecclesisticus 1:14).

From this definition and expansion of the idea of knowledge, we realize that true knowledge, or morality, is based on a right relationship with God. "Fear of the Lord" is the keynote of Old Testament piety. As we have previously seen, "fear of the Lord" is not slavish terror, but rather humility and reverence. There can be no true knowledge, or morality, apart from God and no true ethic apart from respect or reverence for the Lord God.

The word "knowledge" *(daath)* of Proverbs 1:7 has a much richer and deeper meaning than the English word assigns it. In its highest meaning, the Hebrew word for knowledge *(daath)* means a knowledge of God, including total commitment to him. This same word is used by the prophets when they proclaim that the Lord God has rejected his people due to their lack of knowledge (*ie,* lack of faithfulness to the covenant; *cf* Hosea 4:6). The verb form of this word "knowledge" is *yada,* "to know," and is used to express the closest possible human relationship, that of marriage intimacy. For example: "Now Adam knew *(yada)* Eve his wife, and she conceived and bore Cain . . ." (Genesis 4:1). Does not this teach that our relationship with the Lord God should be a close and intimate one? In fact, is not Israel referred to as the bride of the Lord and the New Testament church the bride of Christ?

The purpose of the book of Proverbs is, then, to teach that fear, reverence, and respect for God is the primary aim of man. Such a quest on the part of the young and the wise will result in confidence and trust in the Lord and his covenant promises.

(2) Wisdom's Appeal—In order to attract men to her, Wisdom is personified as a beautiful woman in Proverbs 8:1-11; a woman who freely offers the richness of her gifts. The writer emphasizes that wisdom is of much greater value than any material possession. Neither does wisdom dwell in secrecy and darkness, inaccessible to man, but is found where people are—in the streets, the gates, and the market places. Wisdom is everywhere revealing how trustworthy and precious she is, summoning all classes of people to come to her.

(3) Wisdom's Role in the Universe—Wisdom, the beautiful

woman, is speaking of her origin and part in God's creation in
Proverbs 8:22-36. God is the uncreated Creator and the first thing
he created was Wisdom. Following his creation of Wisdom, God
and Wisdom created the universe and all that is in it.[3] Wisdom's
value is seen in that it was the first thing that God created and was
also his partner in the creation of the universe.

In Proverbs 8:22 the KJV uses the word "possessed" as the
translation of the Hebrew verb, *qānāh*. This Hebrew verb is
translated "created" in the LXX, the Targum, and the Syriac, as
well as in the RSV. *Qānāh* means "to get," or "to acquire," and is
so translated in several passages in Proverbs (*cf* Proverbs 4:5; 7;
15:32; 16:16, 17; etc.). It is translated in relation to God as
"Creator" or "Maker" in Genesis 14:19, 22; Deuteronomy 32:6;
Psalms 139:13. In view of the statement made in the verses
following Proverbs 8:22, concerning Wisdom and the emphasis on
creation, it would seem best to translate *qānāh* as "created" rather
than "possessed." According to the Apocrypha, the Jews of this
period understood that wisdom was created (*cf* Ecclesiasticus 1:4, 9;
24:8; Wisdom of Solomon 7:25).

Other scholars, however, do not agree with the translation
"create" for the Hebrew verb, *qānāh*. Scott writes that "what is
here being affirmed is not that Yahweh is creator, but that Yahweh's
attribute of wisdom 'existed' prior to its expression in his acts of
creation. The meaning 'possess' for *qānāh* is entirely suitable and
is in keeping with the author's usage in 1:5, 4:5, 7. Yahweh
'possessed' wisdom as an attribute or faculty integral to his being
from the very first, and 'in (with, or by) his wisdom founded
the earth' (3:19).[4]

The majority of the early church fathers thought that "wisdom"
of Proverbs 8:22-36 referred to Jesus Christ. Many utilized the
New Testament passages such as John 1:1-4; Colossians 1:15 and
Hebrews 1:3 to support this viewpoint. Is it possible that "wisdom"
of Proverbs 8 refers to Christ as does the "Word" (Greek,
logos) of John 1? Is wisdom a foreshadow of the Son of God? It is
this writer's judgement that "wisdom" and "Word" are not to be
equated for wisdom was "created" whereas Christ has been

---

[3] In Genesis 1:26 the text reads that God said, "Let us make man. . ." Is it possible that God was here speaking to Wisdom?
[4] R. B. Y. Scott, *The Anchor Bible,* Volume 18, *Proverbs, Ecclesiastes* (Garden City, N.Y., 1965), *pp* 71-72.

pre-existent with God from eternity. This thought concerning the possibility of Christ as being "created" led to the fourth century Arian controversy about the nature of the Son of God. Arius contended that since Christ was the "wisdom of God" (1 Corinthians 1:24), he was spoken of in Proverbs as a created being, subordinate to God.

(4) Wisdom's Banquet—The next passage of interest in relation to wisdom is descriptive of wisdom's invitation to a great feast, Proverbs 9:1-6. In the continuing task of revealing the value of acquiring wisdom, the writer utilizes the banquet scene to bring individuals to a higher way of life. Throughout God's word, an invitation to a banquet is used as an illustration of bringing men to God (cf Isaiah 55:1; John 6:35; Revelation 19:9; 22:17).

Wisdom especially speaks to bring the "simple" (vs. 4) to her feast. The "simple" refer, as seen above, to individuals who have not lived or studied long enough to know the way of righteousness, or the way of the "fear of the Lord." The "simple" are those novices who may, with proper instruction and motivation, go on toward the acquisition of true wisdom. Later, we will note that Folly also strives to entice the "simple" to her feast.

According to Proverbs 9:6, if one leaves simpleness of life, he lives. Wisdom is, in fact, called "a tree of life" (Proverbs 3:18) in that she brings the good things of life, the blessings which all men seek—long life, abundance, honor, pleasant ways and peace. Listen to the inspired writer as he elaborates on these themes:

"Length of days is in her right hand;
In her left hand are riches and honor.
Her ways are ways of righteousness,
And all her paths are peace."

—Proverbs 3:16-17

(5) Folly's Banquet—We are now introduced to the second of two powers always striving to win man in Wisdom Literature. That second power is Folly, Proverbs 9:13-18. "Foolish" is the feminine abstract form of "fool" and is the word frequently used in Proverbs to refer to the "foolishness of sin." Folly is the disregard or transgression of the ways of God, which leads to a rash, uncontrolled manner of life. It is a disorder in the center of a man's life which results in misunderstanding of the order in life to which the wise man subordinates himself. Folly is opposed to wisdom and a foolish person is opposite to a wise man. Folly is thus

personified as a harlot and is, therefore, the way of death, or non-wisdom. As does Wisdom, Folly also sits in public places and calls out to the passers-by, urging the inexperienced to "turn in here" (verse 16).

This figure of speech ("harlot" for Folly), in contrast to wisdom (reverence for the Lord), infers the seductive way of life associated with the pagan religions of that day. The figure of marital unfaithfulness is used by many prophets to depict Israel's apostasy into idolatry (cf Hosea 1-3; Jeremiah 2-3; etc.). This figure of sexual indulgence is particularly appropriate because of the practice of cultic prostitution so prevalent in Canaanite religion.

(6) The Reward of A Persistent Search for Wisdom—As was previously discussed, the writers of Wisdom Literature held a strict view of retribution. There is immediate material success for the good life and failure for the wicked. The good man will conduct himself in a right way and will have a long, happy and prosperous life. By contrast, the wicked will suffer hardship and a premature death. Thus, in spite of the high ethical standards set forth in Proverbs, right living is almost always motivated by personal interests or success. This being true, what are some of the rewards of a persistent search for wisdom?

(i) One shall be able to understand wisdom, Proverbs 2:1-9.[5] Throughout this passage of scripture is the admonition to seek diligently for wisdom. If one seeks for wisdom with the diligence of a miner of silver (verse 4) he will be rewarded by an understanding of "righteousness and justice and equity, every good path" (verse 9). In the nation of Brazil, slaves are employed to scrape up the soil from the river bed of the Rio de Janeiro and wash it carefully in order to find particles of gold and diamonds. It is a law of the state that he who finds a diamond of so many carats shall have his freedom. This naturally causes the greatest ardour and diligence in searching and washing. Such is the diligence with which one ought to seek for wisdom (cf Job 28). Every faculty, the ear, the heart, the voice (verses 2-3), must be

[5]"My son" (verse 1) is not necessarily the author's son, but rather a reference to a situation in which an older man is speaking to a younger. The apostle Paul shared this type of relationship with Timothy and Titus (cf 1 Timothy 1:2; 2 Timothy 1:2; Titus 1:4). This word is normally used in Wisdom literature to denote the teacher-student relationship.

employed in the presevering search for wisdom. The ear is to hear the words of wisdom; the heart[6] must be applied and attuned to wisdom; and the voice must cry out for wisdom.

According to Proverbs 2:6, "the Lord gives wisdom." Only here in the book of Proverbs is God, not Wisdom, the teacher and source of wisdom. Proverbs 3:19 reads that "the Lord by wisdom founded the earth," which is indicative that wisdom is *with* God. In fact, wisdom was God's first creation (see Proverbs 8:22 and notes). This being true, wisdom is a gift from God to all men who seek after it.

(ii) One shall be delivered from evil ways (Proverbs 2:10-15). The two most alluring temptations of the Wisdom period of Israel's history appears to have been the temptations to join with evil men, and the temptation to associate with "foolish," or lewd women. Wisdom, therefore, assists the man of wisdom in overcoming such seductive temptations. The wise man, with his God-given wisdom, will be enabled to resist the way of folly, the way of false and destructive attractions. Thus, wisdom gives, not only spiritual and intellectual ability, but also practical insight to the right and the good.

The way of evil is once again described as a "walk in the ways of darkness" (verse 13b). This same description is given in Proverbs 4:18-19:

"The path of the righteous is like the light of dawn,
which shines brighter and brighter until full day.
The way of the wicked is like deep darkness;[7]
they do not know over what they stumble."

The wicked fall because they have no light, but what is worse, they do not know why they fall because they do not recognize wickedness as such. In contrast, wisdom illumines the pathway of the righteous, making them secure in their journey through life.

(iii) One shall be delivered from loose women, Proverbs 2:16-19. Again, wisdom gives one protection from those "loose women," or "adventuresses," who would lure men to their destruction. The

---

[6]Hebrew—*leb;* variously understood as the instrument of man's intellectual and volitional activity; comprehending mind, affections and will.
[7]Hebrew—*aphelah,* not the ordinary word for darkness, but one which means "deep obscurity," or "the entire absence of light."

wise are correctly instructed and so realize they cannot love the way of wisdom and at the same time go after unlawful sexual gratification. The "loose women," or "adventuresses" do not refer, in all probability, to foreign prostitutes in Israel due to the fact that such was forbidden by the law (Leviticus 19:29; 21:9; Deuteronomy 23:17-18). Rather, these women were those who had either divorced their first husband, or those who were guilty of adultery, as seems evident by verse 17. These women had forsaken the companion of their youth[8] and forgotten the covenant[9] of their God.

In verse 17 we note that marriage is not to be viewed as a covenant, or contract, between a man and woman only, but between a man, a woman, and God. Marriage is not a private matter between two consenting adults, and that alone, but a solemn covenant entered into before God. When such a marriage covenant is broken, it implies also the breaking of a covenant with God. Monogamy is taken as the rule, or standard, in Proverbs, and the high and sacred character of marriage and the family is upheld throughout the book.

Proverbs 2:18-19 teaches, as does the apostle Paul, that "the wages of sin is death" (cf Romans 6:23). Those who "go into"[10] loose women will find that such a road leads to death, or Sheol.[11] This road to death is a one-way journey for the way of loose women and all who associate with them are on the way to destruction. As Chrysostom says, "It is as difficult to bring back a libidinous person to chastity as a dead man to life."

(iv) One shall be given an abundant life (Proverbs 3:13-18). In a very impressive commendation of wisdom, designed to enhance the desirability of wisdom, the Proverb writer reveals that the abundant life, the life of honor, peace, happiness, wealth and longevity, belongs not in the material realm, but in the search for and discovery of wisdom. From this we note that wisdom, as set forth in

---

[8]Her husband; cf Malachi 2:14. The Lord applies this phrase to himself and the spiritually adulterous Judah in Jeremiah 3:4.

[9]Her marriage covenant; cf Malachi 2:14.

[10]Hebrew—ba'eyha, a sexual term, as in Genesis 19:34; 2 Samuel 11:4, and rarely used with the woman as the subject.

[11]The punishment here is not eternal torment, but premature, or untimely, death, for the idea of punishment or reward beyond the grave had not yet become prevalent in Hebrew thinking at this time.

48

the scriptures, is both religious and practical. It stems from the fear of the Lord, and branches out into all areas of life. Wisdom is superior to silver and fine gold. It is more precious than rubies, and nothing man can desire is worthy to be compared to wisdom, for all other things are fleeting and trivial in comparison. The "tree of life" (verse 18) is a traditional figure in the scriptures for health and long life (cf Genesis 2:9; 3:22, 24; Proverbs 11:30; 13:12; 15:4; Ezekiel 47:12; Revelation 2:7; 22:2; Ecclesiasticus 24:12-17). It symbolizes "all that is beautiful, all that is desirable, all that gives joy and intensity to living."[12]

Our introduction to the way of Wisdom and the way of Folly closes and we turn now to the study of some general topics of Proverbs. Wisdom and Folly have each spoken and invited. Their rewards and fruits are open for all to see. The reader is now left to seek out, in general daily life, the way of wisdom or the way of Folly. In this study of general topics, the reader will note that Wisdom has to do with the whole of life, and is occupied with all its departments. "Both wisdom and folly are personal philosophies, different ways of looking upon life. Wisdom is the way of the religious man, and it leads to victory; Folly is the way of the impious, and its end is defeat."[13]

GOD

For the religious man, there is evidence that leads him to conclude that God is. To admit God's existence and stop there, however, is not enough. To look at the universe and say, "There must be a God," and then to say, "We can know nothing of him," is to come away with no God at all. We need to know something about this God we say exists, or his existence is worse than no existence at all. We ask, therefore, "What can man know of God?" Here is a question that reveals the longing in men's hearts for a clearer and fuller revelation of the Creator of life. Man desires to have the nature of God clarified and to understand the meaning and relevance of God for life. It is as Augustine said, "Thou madest us for

---

[12]E. Johnson, *The Pulpit Commentary,* Volume 9, *Proverbs* (Grand Rapids, 1962), p. 75. Used by permission of the publisher, Eerdmans Publishing Co.
[13]S. H. Blank, "Folly," *The Interpreter's Dictionary of the Bible,* 1962, Volume 2, 304.

Thyself, and our heart is restless, until it repose in thee."[14] This same inquiry into God is also posed by the writer of Proverbs 30:4:

> "Who has ascended to heaven and come down?
> Who has gathered the wind in his fists?
> Who has wrapped up the waters in a garment?
> Who has established the ends of the earth?
> What is his name, and what is his son's name?
> Surely you know!"

The man of humility and wisdom is aware of his ignorance of God and God's ways. He knows he is not the Creator and as a creature cannot fathom the intentions of the God who made him. He recognizes that God stands over against him as his Creator and over against the world as its Creator. He knows God to be greater than (more than) his creation, the source from which all else flows.

All Christians concede that there is a God in whom "we live and move and have our being" (Acts 17:28). Christians know, too, that God is like Jesus Christ for Jesus came to reveal the Father to man (cf John 8:58; 10:30). God is not just a Being who exists but One who has been revealed. In Christ men were brought into a direct and immediate relationship to God. But is God living and active? What has God done; what does he do; and what, if anything, is he doing right now? Is he alive and active in this world? These are some of the questions we may ask about God as we approach the book of Proverbs. Proverbs reveals that God is not just Being; he is Being who is represented in one way or another so that we may know about him.

(1) The Nature of God—What can we know about the nature of God from a study of Proverbs? We know that God exists, but what do we know of his nature? What does he do and what does he know? "God càn be known indeed," says Thomas of Aquanias, in a natural way "through the images of His effects,"[15] in that these effects are a reflection of him. Although Proverbs was written to glorify Wisdom and warn men against Folly, God's nature is revealed in many images. These images of God's nature reflected in the book of Proverbs are as follows:

---

[14]A. Augustine, *The Confessions of Augustine,* trans. Edward B. Pusey (New York: MacMillian, Co., 1961), VII, 5.
[15]*Summa Theol.,* Ia, q. 13, a. 5; q. 12, a. 12.

(i) God completely controls history—"The king's heart is a stream of water in the hand of the Lord" (Proverbs 21:1). As a farmer directs a stream of water to whatever part of the land he chooses by opening a particular irrigation gate, so the Lord God directs the kings of the earth to accomplish his designs. The king is subject to God for God has complete control over the plans and decisions of the king by divine influences and intercessions into history. The king's rule, therefore, is one of success and endurance when he subjects himself to this counsel of God. This absolute trust in God was most vividly characterized in the life-style of Jesus: "Father, into thy hands I commit my spirit" (Luke 23:46). Being subject to the laws and control of God, the king must responsibly use the powers given to him by God (*cf* Proverbs 19:21; 20:27-28; Job 12:24-25).

This control of God over history is revealed outside the book of Proverbs in many examples. One such example is 2 Samuel 8, which details David's great victories in battle. The inspired record informs the reader that David overpowered the Syrians, the Edomites, the Philistines, and so forth. The record could have stated that David was victorious due to his strong army, or good leadership, but it does not. Rather it states, in a matter of fact manner, "the *Lord* gave victory to David wherever he went" (2 Samuel 8:14b). The secret of his success was that he was being guarded and directed by God. God's nature is such that he completely controls history.

The Proverb writer also states that, "No wisdom, no understanding, no counsel, can avail against the Lord" (Proverbs 21:30). Wisdom as used here means the arrogant claim of secular wisdom (*cf* Job 5:12-13; 12:2; 28:13; 39:19-30; 1 Corinthians 1:20). No human wisdom can avail against God. Acknowledgment of this fact will assist a man in not thinking more highly of himself than he ought to think. Even the highest ruler of the land is a creature and cannot equate his opinions and judgments with those of the Lord God. The major problem with man is that he prefers to walk by his own wisdom. God, however, entered the world with its false wisdom and introduced his wisdom, which is contrary to the wisdom of the world. God's wisdom melts away human pride and results in trusting humility and true wisdom.

(ii) God's nature is such that he knows the hearts of men—"The eyes of the Lord are in every place, keeping watch on the evil and the good. . . . Sheol and Abaddon[16] lie open before the Lord, how much more the hearts of men" (Proverbs 15:3, 11). The emphasis in these two verses is that God is keeping watch over the good and the bad, and, therefore, will punish the wicked and reward the righteous. His eyes penetrate even the most secret corners of the unseen world and if he knows the secrets of the hidden places beyond the grave, how much more does he know the hearts of men? Such omniscience and omnipresence on the part of God is alarming to the evil doers but a source of great comfort to the man of Wisdom, for it reveals a Creator who is concerned for his creatures.

The interest of God for his creatures is revealed in the fact that he knows everything about his creatures. This activity of God in man's experience is shown very clearly in Psalm 139. The Psalmist teaches that God not only knows everything about man, but that God cares for him and considers the smallest details of his life, even the purposes of his mind. Out of a full heart the Psalmist prays:

> O Lord, thou hast searched me and known me!
> Thou knowest when I sit down and when I rise up;
> thou discernest my thoughts from afar.
> Thou searchest out my path and my lying down,
> and art acquainted with all my ways.
> Even before a word is on my tongue,
> lo, O Lord, thou knowest it altogether.
> Thou dost beset me behind and before,
> and layest thy hand upon me.
> Such knowledge is too wonderful for me;
> it is high, I cannot attain it.
>
> Psalm 139:1-6

God's nature is such that he knows the hearts of men, and this should not bring to man a feeling of imprisonment or death, but freedom and life, for our God is a God of love and concern. Our God is a shepherd who leaves the flock to search for one stray, in order to bring it back to warmth and safety. Our God is like the father who welcomes the prodigal son with open arms. Our God is

---

[16]The KJV uses "Hell" and "destruction" for these two Hebrew words, *sheol* and *abaddon*. Such a translation views these places as the abode of the damned, like the Greek *tartaroo*. But again, we note that Sheol and Abaddon are none other than the place of the dead and of destruction, not eternal torment, or Hell (*cf* Psalms 88:11; Job 28:22; 31:12).

the Father who wins our love and allegiance from the cruel cross of his Son. We too can say with the Psalmist: "I praise thee, for thou are fearful and wonderful. Wonderful are thy works! Thou knowest me right well" (Psalms 139:14).

(iii) God's nature is such that he is more concerned with righteousness than with sacrifice—"To do righteousness and justice is more acceptable to the Lord than sacrifice" (Proverbs 21:3). This thought is the same as 1 Samuel 15:22, which has reference to King Saul: "And Samuel said, 'Has the Lord as great delight in burnt offerings and sacrifices, as in obeying the voice of the Lord? Behold, to obey is better than sacrifice and to hearken than the fat of rams.' " This emphasis was also the major emphasis in the message of the eighth century prophets (cf Amos 5:22-24; Hosea 6:6; Micah 6:6-8; Isaiah 1:10-17; Jeremiah 6:20; etc.). The implication here is that equitable and righteous dealings in relation to God and man must proceed from the heart of love and not from bare regard to the law. The outward and inward aspect of the religious life must be in harmony for the life of worship to be of value. No measure of outward observance can overcome the lack of inward morality and commitment.

This emphasis on righteousness and justice is not meant to infer that God is not interested in his covenant people keeping the laws respecting the sacrificial system. Rather it is that at all times sacrifices are subordinate to the spirit in which they are offered. Keeping the law is important, but it is without benefit if the worshipper's heart is not attuned to God. Righteousness and justice are more important in God's sight than ritual correctness. As the Proverb writer says, "The sacrifices of the wicked is an abomination to the Lord, but the prayer of the upright is his delight" (Proverbs 15:8). Sacrifices that are pleasing to the Lord, and worship that is pleasing to the Lord, are the sacrifices and worship from a heart and life in harmony with the Lord's will.

The proverbs concerning the superior value of righteousness and justice over sacrifices have special significance if they come from the pen of Solomon, for we read that "King Solomon and all the congregation of Israel, who has assembled before him, were with him before the ark, sacrificing so many sheep and oxen that they could not be counted or numbered" (1 Kings 8:5). Solomon's one great commission in life was the completion of the temple in Jerusalem where sacrifice would be offered to the Lord. In the midst of this emphasis on sacrifices, this proverb would indeed be a wise admonition to the people of God.

(iv) God's nature is such that he hates wickedness—"The way of the wicked is an abomination to the Lord, but he loves him who pursues righteousness" (Proverbs 15:9). Here, as in the New Testament (cf Acts 9:2; 19:9; 19:23; 24:22), the manner and rule of life is referred to as "the way." The way of life that is acceptable to the Lord is correct religious practice coupled with right living. As sacrifice without righteousness is not acceptable to the Lord, so also is the correct worship separated from righteous living not acceptable.

A deeper incentive than self-interest must be at work, however, if true moral righteousness is to be achieved. The godly man must be motivated to do good not only in order to be blessed by God, but also because doing good is to be like God. The necessity of being motivated to righteousness by something other than selfish considerations is vividly illustrated in the old legend about an elderly woman who was seen in the streets of Strasbourg in the fourteenth century. When seen, the woman was carrying a pan of water in one hand and a torch in the other. "When asked what she was about, she answered that with the pail of water she was going to put out the flames of hell and with the torch she was going to burn up heaven, so that in the future men would love the dear Lord God for himself alone and not out of fear of hell or out of craving for reward."[17]

(2) God is Creator—As noted earlier, wisdom was the first of God's creative acts and thus became a fellow-creator with God (Proverbs 8:22-36). The writers of Proverbs were not content to affirm that blind chance had produced this universe of ours. Religious faith comes to rest by saying that, "In the beginning God created the heaven and the earth" (Genesis 1:1). Genesis gives a marvelous account of the creation of the world, and although cast in a poetic form, not one word contradicts the most certain of modern scientific truths. The religious man is willing to use the word "God" as a name for that which has always existed and has brought into being all that comprises the heavens and the earth. Even Darwin said that the universe is "that grand sequence of events which the mind refuses to accept as the result of blind chance."[18]

---

[17]Douglas V. Steere, *Prayer and Worship* (Wallingford, Pa., 1938), *p* 11.
[18]Quoted from W. Macneile Dixon, *The Human Situation* (New York, 1937), *p* 318.

54

In relation to the creation, the Proverb writer states, "The Lord
by wisdom founded the earth; by understanding he established the
heavens; by his knowledge the deep broke forth, and the clouds
drop down the dew" (Proverbs 3:19-20). With this verse the writer
reveals that wisdom, which directs human life toward God, is the
same wisdom by which God created the heavens and the earth
(cf Isaiah 40:12-14, 28; Jeremiah 10:13; Psalms 104:24; 136:5;
Job 9:10; 38-39). To surrender one's life to wisdom would, then,
result in harmony between man and the world which surrounds
him. The individual who chooses to leave the circle of existence that
God planned for him seeks after a different wisdom and, thus,
finds himself separated from nature, self and God. Seeking after
the wisdom of God, however, results in an overcoming of these
separations and a greater wholeness in life.

Two phenomena of nature are ascribed to God in Proverbs 3:20:
"The deeps broke forth" refers to the separation of the waters
from the earth at the time of the creation (Genesis 1:9), or to the
subterranean waters released at the time of the flood of Noah's
day (Genesis 7:11). The second phenomena, "The clouds drop down
the dew," refers to the precipitation as the earth is refreshed from
above. According to Micah 5:7, such precipitation was considered
a precious gift of the Lord, especially in the dry climate of Palestine.
Thus, the wise man attributes these two effects, the subterranean
and the higher waters, to the wisdom and control of God.

God's creation is not a creation of discrimination for all men,
regardless of their social status, are from God: "The rich and the
poor meet together; the Lord is the maker of them all" (Proverbs
22:2). The man of God must manifest concern for his fellow man.
Indifference toward others is displeasing to the Lord. In *David
Copperfield*, Miss Dartle welcomed the suggestion of Steerforth
that poor people were not as sensitive as other people: "It's so
consoling! It's such a delight to know that, when they suffer, they
don't feel! Sometimes I have been quite uneasy for that sort of
people; but now I shall just dismiss the idea of them altogether.
Live and learn."[19] So many times we avoid our responsibility
toward others because they are of no advantage to us. The writer
of Proverbs reflects this common tendency among men: "All a
poor man's brothers hate[20] him; how much more do his friends go

[19]David Copperfield, chapter XX.
[20]Hebrew, *sane*—"fail in concern for."

far from him" (Proverbs 19:7).

One day a lawyer stood up to test Jesus and said, "Who is my neighbor?" (Luke 10:29). Jesus responded to this question by telling the parable of the Good Samaritan and once and for all revealed to man that his neighbor is every man. We realize, even within our own lives, that this limitation of love due to color, race, or social position, is not yet absent. Our responsibility toward others, however, is not a question of who is next to us socially, or physically, but of all who need us and of where we will go and what we will do in answer to the needs of our fellow creatures. Josiah manifested this concern and was praised by the Lord: "He judged the cause of the poor and needy; then it was well. Is not this to know me? says the Lord" (Jeremiah 22:16). Being concerned with the poor and needy was in itself a knowing of the Lord.

God's concern is not just with the poor and needy, however, for he causes his light to shine on all classes of men: "The poor man and the oppressor meet together; the Lord gives light to the eyes of both" (Proverbs 29:13). Our common humanity, our fatherhood in God, ought to make us regard one another as brethren, without distinction of rank or position. The well-to-do must not despise the poor man, nor should the poor envy and hate the rich (*cf* Proverbs 3:31; 14:31; 17:5; Job 31:15). The intermingling of the diversities of men is for the end that the exalted and the lowly should have a care and concern for one another. Personal worth is of far greater value than any wealth or lack of wealth.

In relation to the created world, we often take for granted the things that God has wisely made. For example, "The hearing ear and the seeing eye, the Lord has made them both" (Proverbs 20:12). Men ought to appreciate and use the ear and the eye in conformity with the design which they are intended to serve, that is, lend the ear to instruction (Proverbs 18:15), and keep the eye open to observe (Proverbs 20:13). Chrysostom wrote,

> God hath given us eyes, not that we may look wantonly, but that, admiring his handiwork, we may worship the Creator. And that this is the use of our eyes is evident from the things which are seen. For the lustre of the sun and of the sky we see from an immeasurable distance, but a woman's beauty one cannot discern so far off. Seest thou that for this end our eye was chiefly given? Again, he made the ear, that we should entertain not blasphemous words, but saving doctrines.

Wherefore you see, when it receives anything dissonant, both our soul shudders and our very body also. And if we hear anything cruel or merciless, again our flesh creeps; but if anything decorous and kind, we even exult and rejoice.[21]

(3) God is the Supreme Ruler—If God is supreme ruler, then, he is concerned with everything which he made. In Proverbs 16 we read: "The plans of the mind belong to man, but the answer of the tongue is from the Lord. . . . The Lord has made everything for its purpose, even the wicked for the day of trouble. . . . A man's mind plans his way, but the Lord directs his steps. . . . The lot is cast into the lap, but the decision is wholly from the Lord" (verses 1, 4, 9, 33; cf Proverbs 19:21; 21:30-31; Matthew 10:19-20). Man has great freedom and his mind plans his way, but man's decisions are not necessarily in harmony with the designs of God. A popular proverb is, "Man proposes, God disposes." Everything in God's creation has its own end and object and reason for being and, therefore, is being properly utilized only when it is being used in harmony with God's revealed will.

The reference to casting lots (Proverbs 16:33) reflects a common method the Jews used to make a decision. They believed the resultant decision was directly from the Lord. This method was used by the Jews from the time of Joshua to the early days of the Christian faith (Leviticus 16:8; Numbers 26:55; Joshua 18:10; Judges 20:9; 1 Samuel 10:20-21; Jonah 1:7; Psalms 22:18; Acts 1:26; etc). Lot casting was not blind superstition either, for the Jews did not resort to casting lots for every trivial reason. The casting of lots was employed religiously in cases where other means were not suitable or available. It was not to supercede common prudence or careful investigation, but rather was used in situations where the deciding evidence was conflicting and there resulted great indecision in making judgment. Thus, Proverbs 18:18: "The lot puts an end to disputes and decides between powerful contenders."

The passages relating to God's control over the purposes of man (Proverbs 16:1, 4, 9, 33; etc.), have been used by those who teach the doctrine of predestination,[22] the idea that before the creation of

---

[21]*Hom.* xxii in 1 Corinthians

[22]One of the most celebrated proof-texts of the predestinationists is Isaiah 45:7: "I make peace and create evil." In this passage, "evil" (Hebrew—*ra*) means "evil, distress, calamity, or misery." In contrast with "peace," *ra* must mean "calamity."

the world, God determined all that would come to pass in it. These verses do not teach the doctrine of predestination. They simply teach that nothing, including the wicked, shall escape the control and judgment of God. In saying that God made "even the wicked for the day of trouble" (Proverbs 16:4), the writer does not mean that God made the wicked to be wicked, but that he made the wicked as he made all others, that is, with the powers and capacities to use for good or for evil. Man is created in God's image and, as such, has the freedom to choose the direction of his life.

God's will, therefore, is to use man's lifestyle for his purposes and to promote his glory. This is seen in the situations with Pharaoh, Nebuchadnezzar, Judas Iscariot, and countless others. In reference to Pharaoh (Exodus 9:16), the apostle Paul explains (Romans 9) that it was not Pharaoh's conduct that determined the will of God, but that the will of God is always antecedent of any conduct on man's part. Nothing happens to God through the obstinacy and rebellion of man which determines God to an action not already embraced in his eternal plan. The apostle Paul adds: "What if God, desiring to show his wrath and to make known his power, has endured with much patience the vessels of wrath made for destruction, in order to make known the riches of his glory . . . (Romans 9:22-23). Paul recognizes the factor of human self-determination, but he recognizes it as one comprehended in the plan of God.

(4) God is the Judge and Rewarder of Human Action—"All the ways of a man are pure in his own eyes, but the Lord weighs the spirit. . . . When a man's ways please the Lord, he makes even his enemies to be at peace with him" (Proverbs 16:2, 7). The standards of man are to be tested by the Lord. ". . . to weigh the spirit" is an idiom derived ultimately from the religious beliefs of ancient Egypt, in which judgment after death followed the weighing of a man's heart against truth. God will judge, not only the ways of man, but also his spirit, the inner desires and motives. Man's inner motive, or spirit, is the thing that distinguishes him as a man. In the Sermon on the Mount, Jesus deals with this same principle (Matthew 5:21-22, 27). The apostle John also: "Any one who hates

---

Thus, the reference is not to the idea that God might create men that will be predestined to evil, but that God will create misery, or woe, for those in the world who choose to do evil and not good. Thus, the RSV translation, "I make weal and create woe" (Isaiah 45:7).

his brother is a murderer" (1 John 3:15). While the human law considers only overt acts, God considers the motives in one's inner life, for this is where all the outward acts of hatred, violence and wickedness originate. Man may deceive himself, be unperceptive to his own thoughts, or even be uninformed, yet God will judge man's situation in light of his truth.

The idea of God as the Judge and Rewarder of human action is also set forth by the apostle Paul: "I am not aware of anything against myself, but I am not thereby acquitted. It is the Lord who judges me" (1 Corinthians 4:4). Many times man is blind to his personal faults, or he plays them down. The adulterer, or the alcoholic, is not welcomed into the fellowship of the community very easily, whereas the gossiper, or liar, or man dishonest in his business dealings, are welcomed and often seen as pillars of the community. Men have the tendency to like and associate with those who sin as they sin. God is, by way of contrast, the Judge and will determine the action of all men and reward without discrimination.

"When a man's ways please the Lord, he makes even his enemies to be at peace with him" (Proverbs 16:7). This is one of the great promises in the Word of God. Experience proves that nothing succeeds like righteous living and when a man is righteous and devotes himself to seeing good, even his enemies have the tendency to become his friends. Goodness has the power to disarm opposition and promote peace and harmony. This verse could also mean that God is pleased with a righteous person who is able to live righteously and at the same time be at peace with his enemies. If this interpretation is correct, the "he" of "he makes his enemies to be at peace," would refer to the person living righteously.

God, as Rewarder, also determines what reward man needs. From time to time man needs testing: "The crucible is for silver, and the furnace is for gold, and the Lord tries hearts" (Proverbs 17:3). As heat brings out the true nature of precious metals, so God tries the hearts of men in order to bring out their true character. Such trials or testing will reveal the true character of one's life, whether it be a life of obedience and trust, or a life that is shallow and unstable. The testing is not for this alone, however, but also for purifying and maturing, for developing one's character. True character is more valuable than gold and silver, therefore, if man tests these metals, how much more will God test man's character.

The apostle Peter taught this same truth: "In this (the hope we have in Christ) you rejoice, though now for a little while you may have to suffer various trials, so that the genuineness of your faith, more precious than gold which though perishable is tested by fire, may redound to praise the glory and honor at the revelation of Jesus Christ" (1 Peter 1:6-7). We must not think we are forgotten by God when faced with trials, nor should we regard such trials as a limitation of God's power, love or concern. Rather, we should view such trials as opportunities to demonstrate the quality and reality of our faith. Our faith must be of such a nature that it remains unshaken in the midst of difficult times. Our faith can remain unshaken for the apostle Paul assures us, "No temptation[23] has overtaken you that is not common to man. God is faithful, and he will not let you be tempted beyond your strength, but with the temptation will also provide the way of escape, that you may be able to endure it" (1 Corinthians 10:13).

(5) God is the Enemy of All Forms of Evil—Proverbs 6:16 says that God "hates." We are so accustomed to hearing and reading of God's love and of God as a friend that it is shocking to hear and read of God hating, or of God being an enemy, yet this is precisely what God is and manifests toward certain things. There are some things that God hates, that are an abomination to him, because of what they are and what they do to his children and his purposes. What are some of the specific evils mentioned in Proverbs that God is hostile toward?

(i) Disobedience—"If one turns away his ear from hearing the law, even his prayer is an abomination" (Proverbs 28:9; cf Proverbs 1:24; Isaiah 66:4; Jeremiah 7:13). In earlier literature "abomination" referred to something which was contrary to the religious cult, but later on, as here, it referred to moral offenses. There may be forebearance on the part of God for ignorance, as some passages in the New Testament seem to indicate(cf Acts 3:17; 17:30), but when a man has the opportunity to know and do the will of God, yet rejects it due to self-will and rebellion, he receives unto himself the disfavor of God. Once again the emphasis is directed to the fact that God demands obedience and right living as well as right prayer (cf Proverbs 15:8; 1 Samuel 15:22). To devote one's attention to self-centered values will be to reap the fleeting and hollow values of

---

[23]Greek—*peirasmos*—"test, trial, temptation, enticement." This word is used in 1 Peter 1:6; James 1:2, and 1 Corinthians 10:13.

60

the world as well as the wrath of God.

(ii) Pride— "Every one who is arrogant is an abomination to the Lord; be assured, he will not go unpunished" (Proverbs 16:5). "A man's pride will bring him low, but he who is lowly in spirit will obtain honor" (Proverbs 29:23). Pride toward God is the ultimate sin for it is the assumption on the part of man that he is self-sufficient and that his importance is significant enough for him to demand a place of great prestige (cf Proverbs 15:33; 16:18; 25:6, 14; 26:12; 27:2; 30:13; etc). Pride opposes the first principle of wisdom, the fear of the Lord. Pride also violates the first commandment for it is idolatry—the effort to found life upon man and the finite rather than the infinite. C. S. Lewis wrote:

> "There is one vice in which no man in the world is free; which every one in the world loathes when he sees it in someone else; and of which hardly any people, except Christians, ever imagine that they are guilty themselves. I have heard people admit that they are bad-tempered, or that they cannot keep their heads about girls and drink, or even that they are cowards. I do not think I have ever heard anyone who was not a Christian accuse himself of this vice. And at the same time I have very seldom met anyone, who was not a Christian, who showed the slightest mercy to it in others. There is no fault which makes a man more unpopular, and no fault which we are more unconscious of in ourselves. And the more we have it in ourselves, the more we dislike it in others. . . . The vice I am talking of is Pride of Self-Conceit: and the virtue opposite to it, in Christian morals, is called Humility. . . . According to Christian teachers, the essential vice, the utmost evil, is Pride. Unchastity, anger, greed, drunkenness, and all that, are mere fleabites in comparison: it was through Pride that the devil became the devil: Pride leads to every other vice: it is the complete anti-God state of mind."[24]

It is evident that Proverbs has a lot to say about pride and, thus, we realize the dangers of this grave sin. It leads to strife, warfare, and finally self-destruction: "Pride goes before destruction, and a haughty spirit before a fall. . . . Before destruction a man's heart is haughty" (Proverbs 16:18; 18:12). In Proverbs 6:16-19, the writer

[24]C. S. Lewis, *Mere Christianity* (New York, 1960), *pp* 108-09.

lists seven destestable qualities which the Lord God hates. The "six" and "seven" is a common Hebrew teaching method used throughout the Old Testament (*cf* Proverbs 30:15, 18, 24; Amos 1-2; Job 5:19). Here the writer lists six abominable qualities with the seventh being the worst of all. Thus, pride is the most detestable of things in the sight of God. This is why the Talmud reads: "Of every proud man God says, He and I cannot live in the world together." The wise man, therefore, commends the individual who walks humbly with God and who refuses to be haughty in spirit toward others.

(iii) A person who worships with evil intentions—"The sacrifices of the wicked is an abomination; how much more when he brings it with evil intent" (Proverbs 21:27). The thought here seems to be that of bringing an offering to God in order to win his approval or to try and compensate for one's transgressions. Delitzsch wrote that such sacrifices "are to God a twofold and a threefold abomination; for in this case not only does the godless fail in respect of repentance and a desire after salvation, which are the conditions of all sacrifices acceptable to God, but he makes God directly a minister of sin."[25] This reminds one of the gangster days of the 1920's in the United States when hoods would rob and murder and yet make grand donations to the Church as if they could, by this generosity, be absolved from guilt. The old proverb, "steal the goose, and give the giblets in alms," remains a very prevalent temptation.

In the Sermon on the Mount Jesus relates the necessity of being reconciled to one's brother prior to worshipping in an acceptable manner (Matthew 5:21-26). This teaching is applicable to this situation also for it is impossible to maintain right worship with God if one is not at peace with his fellow man. God continually judges the inner motive of his people. Man, in order to be pleasing to God, must worship in spirit and in truth, and live out in day to day activities the type of life professed in worship.

(iv) Injustice in business—"Diverse weights and diverse measures are both alike an abomination to the Lord" (Proverbs 20:10; *cf* Proverbs 11:1; 16:11; 20:23). This sin was like placing a thumb on the scale while weighing, or the over-pricing of merchandise. There

---

[25]F. Delitzsch, *Keil Delitzsch Commentary on the Old Testament,* Volume VI, *Proverbs, Ecclesiastes, Song of Solomon* (Grand Rapids, 1973), *p* 80. Used by permission of the publisher, Eerdmans Publishing Co.

were various methods used in ancient Israel by unethical merchants to cheat customers. One method was the falsely graduated balance. Another was to have shekel weights of varying weights to be used to one's own advantage in buying and selling. Stones were also used as standards of weight and these could be chipped or grounded off to weigh less. Such dishonesty was strictly forbidden by the law of Moses: "You shall do no wrong in judgment, in measures of length or weight or quantity. You shall have just balances, just weights, a just ephah, and a just hin . . ." (Leviticus 19:35-36; cf Deuteronomy 25:15). Honesty in business was a major concern for the Lord, and in the days of the eighth century prophets this was a major sin of Israel (cf Ezekiel 45:10; Hosea 12:7; Amos 8:5; Micah 6:11). As in religious life, honesty and integrity are at the foundation of economic and social life also. Thus, dishonest merchants were continually under attack by the lawmakers, prophets and wise men of Israel.

Some connect Proverbs 20:10 with the preceding verse, "Who can say, 'I have made my heart clean; I am pure from my sin'?" (Proverbs 20:9), and say that the writer is concerned, not with economic dealings, but rather with the temptation and habit of measuring a neighbor by higher standards than one applies to himself. It is so easy to point out the faults and short-comings of others, especially when we expect others to live up to standards we do not even set for ourselves.

(v) A person who sows discord among brethren—"There are six things which the Lord hates, seven which are an abomination to him: haughty eyes, a lying tongue, and hands that shed innocent blood, a heart that devises wicked plans, feet that make haste to run to evil, a false witness who breathes out lies, and a man who sows discord among brothers" (Proverbs 6:16-19). A person who sows discord is the seventh thing in the list of sins which the Lord hates, therefore, it is the most detestable of them all. In contrast, Jesus taught, "Blessed are the peacemakers" (Matthew 5:9). There is a great need for those who actively promote peace and good will, who do not repeat words which should have been allowed to pass by unnoticed, and who do not thrive on tension and sarcasm. How valuable are Paul's words to Corinth: "I appeal to you, brethren, by the name of our Lord Jesus Christ, that all of you agree and that there is no dissensions among you, but that you be united in the same mind and the same judgment" (1 Corinthians 1:10).

(6) God Is the Champion of the Needy and the Faithful—the nature of God is such that he has concern for the needy, the poor, and the orphans. One kind of dishonesty practiced in ancient Israel was the removing or shifting of landmarks so as to change the boundaries of property. In those days when it was not possible to permanently fix the boundaries, or to keep definitive records, the changing or destroying of landmarks was a most serious offense. Clarke wrote: "Even among the heathens the landmark was sacred; so sacred that they made a deity of it. *Terminus* signifies the stone or post that served as a landmark. And *Terminus* was reputed a god, who had offerings made to him."[26] "The Lord tears down the house of the proud, but maintains a widow's boundaries" (Proverbs 15:25). This same warning is given again: "Do not remove an ancient landmark or enter the fields of the fatherless; for their Redeemer is strong; he will plead their cause against you" (Proverbs 23:10-11). Even the law of Moses called for severe punishment against those who removed landmarks which were set up to prevent the poor from being encroached upon (*cf* Deuteronomy 25:5-10; 27:17). The story of Naboth and his vineyard (1 Kings 21) illustrates these proverbs and laws, but does not limit them just to boundaries for they are relevant to all kinds of exploitation. While the Old Testament does not condemn wealth and material goods, it deals strongly with those who deal with the poor and defenseless in deceit and injustice.

God is referred to in Proverbs 23:10-11 as "Redeemer" (Hebrew—*goel*),[27] originally the next of kin who avenges the estate of the dead kinsman, or who raises up posterity for him" (*cf* Deuteronomy 25:5-10; Ruth 2:20; 3:9; 4:4-6; Leviticus 25:25; Numbers 5:8). The redeemer was also the kinsmen who came to the rescue of one who had fallen into slavery or oppression (*cf* Leviticus 25:48; Proverbs 23:10-11). Here, the thought seems to be that as destitute as the poor, the orphans, and the widows might be, there is one who claims them as next of kin and will defend them, that individual being the Lord God. Thus God will champion the rights of the poor and helpless, and he will help those who cannot help themselves.

---

[26]Adam Clarke, *Clarke's Commentary,* Volume 3, *Job—Song of Solomon* (Nashville, *nd*), p 766.
[27]God is referred to as "Redeemer" in Genesis 48:16; Exodus 6:6; Job 19:25; Isaiah 41-63.

64

"Do not rob the poor,[28] because he is poor, or crush the afflicted at the gate; for the Lord will plead their cause and despoil of life those who despoil them" (Proverbs 22:22-23). "Gate" was the place at the city walls where the elders sat in judgment on cases. In that day, as in ours, it was easy for the poor to be defeated because they were being challenged by men of substance. Once again, however, God assures that he will plead for and defend the poor. Immanuel Kant saw in this relationship between persons an unconditional command: "So act as to treat humanity, whether in thine own person or in that of any other, in every case as an end withal, never as means only."[29] Is not this ideal so richly expressed by Jesus? "You shall love your neighbor as yourself" (Matthew 22:39). Our fellow men are not objects to be used to further our ends, rather they are fellow-creatures made in the image of God.

MAN

What does the book of Proverbs have to say about man? The modern optimistic view of man, based on Greek Aristotelianism and medieval Thomism, is that man is a "spark" of the Absolute Spirit, inherently immortal, ethically good, or at least neutral, and destined by evolution to self-perfection and complete union with the divine. In contrast, the contemporary pessimistic view of man is set forth by Feuerback: *"Der Mensch ist was er essr"*—"Man is what he eats." This view receives characteristic expression in the despair of the modern existentialism set forth by Heideggar: man is "being unto death," or as Sarte: "Man is a useless passion."

The biblical view of man is more balanced than either of the two above views, however. Man is not a complicated being needing only time and opportunity to reach perfection, nor is he a being on the way to a tragic destiny. The biblical interpretation of man is that he is an individual who lives in daily tension between the tragic perversions of what he might have been and the glorious foretaste of what he may be, and, in fact, will be with God's grace and power.

The Christian revelation of man is that he was "made a little lower than God" (Hebrew 2:5), crown of the entire creation (Genesis

---

[28]Hebrew—*dal*—"feeble, powerless, lanquid."
[29]Immanuel Kant, *Fundamental Principles of the Metaphysics of Morals,* tr. T. K. Abbott; 6th edition (London, 1909), p. 47.

1:26, 2:3), declared "very good" by God himself, entrusted with possession of the earth (Gensis 1:31), instructed to rule over earthly creatures (Genesis 1:26; Psalms 8), and commanded to subdue earth and its resources for human well being (Genesis 1:28-30). In summation, by contrast with the rest of earth's creation, man was made to be godlike (Genesis 1:26-27), and in personal communion with God (Genesis 3:8). The tragedy of man, however, is that he has fallen from this ideal state in many ways and has become spiritually alienated from God (Isaiah 59:2).

God's will for man is not that man continue in an estranged relationship with himself. God purposed that man's ethical destiny include a complete restoration to his Creator. Such restoration and relationship becomes a reality in Jesus Christ. "For God so loved the world that he gave his only Son, that whoever believes in him should not perish but have eternal life. For God sent the Son into the world, not to condemn the world, but that the world might be saved through him" (John 3:16-17). Man's goal today, therefore, is not a selfish realization of his own potentiality, nor some abstract perfectionism; rather man achieves his ultimate good as the creative Father, in infinite love and wisdom, works out for him and in him what is best for him as a unique individual in Christ. As the apostle Paul says, "We know that in everything God works for good with those who love him, who are called according to his purpose" (Romans 8:28).

Man is, by creation, a social being: "It is not good that man should be alone" (Genesis 2:8). God created man for fellowship with himself, and woman to provide human fellowship for man (cf Genesis 2:18-25; 1 Corinthians 11:9). This intimate circle of family love affords a prototype for all humanity. This being true, how is man to live in this world as a social being? What does the book of Proverbs tell us about man and his life in God's world?

(1) The Nature of Man—As has been discussed above, man is created in the image of God. This fact is clearly evident by several scriptures, but is not precisely explained (cf Genesis 1:26-27; 5:1; 9:6; 1 Corinthians 11:7; James 3:9). Something of an explanation of man's nature occurs in two New Testament passages. In Colossians 3:10 Paul urges the Christians to "put on the new nature, which is being renewed in knowledge after the image of its creator." This same apostle urges the Ephesian Christians to "put on the new nature, created after the likeness of God in true righteousness and holiness" (Ephesians 4:24). One may infer from these two scriptures

that the image of God in man consists of knowledge, or rationality, and righteousness, or holiness, from which proceed dominion over the lower creation. These things may be true, but a more practical insight into the nature of man can be gained from the book of Proverbs. At this time we wish to note some of the universal characteristics of man as set forth in Proverbs.

(i) Man's future is uncertain—"Do not boast about tomorrow, for you do not know what a day may bring forth" (Proverbs 27:1; cf James 4:13-15). Here is a reminder, like the one given by Jesus in the parable of the Rich Fool (Luke 12:16-21), that it is God, not man, who directs the course of events in one's life. It would be arrogant and presumptuous to assume otherwise. The life of man is dependent on so many unknown things, and is effected by numerous and complicated circumstances, therefore, there can be no confidence about tomorrow. Thus the apostle Peter, boasting with such confidence in his loyalty to Jesus Christ, fell into the sin of denial of his Lord. The only sure and right thing would be to humbly place one's future in the hand of the eternal God. The boast of one's plans and achievements in lofty self-assurance is to leave God out of one's future, a serious and deadly transgression. Such can be avoided by following the advice of the Psalmist: "Trust in the Lord, and do good" (Psalms 37:31). Man's future is certain only when he trusts in the Lord who holds the future and when he avoids the arrogant temptation to boast in tomorrow.

(ii) Each man thinks that he is right—"Every way of a man is right in his own eyes, but the Lord weighs the heart" (Proverbs 21:2; cf Proverbs 12:15; 16:2). Individuals would not do what they do if they thought it was not the best way, or the best way for them at the particular time or situation. Trimberg says in Remer, "all fools live in the pleasant feeling that their life is the best."[30] The truth of the matter is, however, that man may deceive himself, or be blind to his own faults. He may be following an ill-informed conscience. It must be remembered that it is the Lord who weighs the motives, intentions and dispositions of men. Man must, therefore, continually examine himself and determine that his standard is not his own opinion and wisdom.

"There is a way which seems right to a man, but its end is the way to death" (Proverbs 14:12; cf Proverbs 16:25; 20:24). Appearances

---

[30]Quote taken from: F. Delitzsch, op cit, p. 63.

are often deceitful and, thus, "seeing life through to its end is more than being faithful unto death—it is also the capacity to see the ultimate and logical consequences of a particular course of action."[31] The Proverbs writer emphasizes again the importance of trusting one's way to the Lord. There will be times in one's life when the ways of the Lord seem strange and difficult, but appearances are deceiving. We need to be on guard against the prevalent tendency to succumb to appearances. The Preacher says, "But all this I laid to heart, examining it all, how the righteous and the wise and their deeds are in the hand of God; whether it is love or hate man does not know" (Ecclesiastes 9:1).

(iii) Man is always trying to learn something that he does not know—"Sheol and Abaddon are never satisfied, and never satisfied are the eyes of man" (Proverbs 27:20). This passage is internal emblematic parallelism (the use of a simile—"as" or "like"). Death is never satisfied for people keep on dying no matter how full the graves get. In like manner the eyes of man are never satisfied. Man is always seeking to do, have or know something new. As the Preacher says, "The eye is not satisfied with seeing" (Ecclesiastes 1:8). Again we are reminded that man will never be satisfied by the temporal things of the world. Seeking satisfaction in such results is an ever-widening and useless search for new things. The solution to such a fruitless search is found in the words of Jesus Christ: "But seek first his kingdom and his righteousness, and all these things shall be yours as well" (Matthew 6:33). The spirit of man, created in God's image, can only find satisfaction in union with its Creator. Augustine taught this truth so well when he said, "O God, thou hast made us for thyself, and our heart findeth no rest until it resteth in thee."

(iv) Man weeps and rejoices alone—"The heart knows its own bitterness, and no stranger shares its joy" (Proverbs 14:10). An old proverb in harmony with this one is: "everyone knows where his shoe pinches." A most difficult thing to do is to share in one's sorrow or happiness, for a man's most inward feelings are known only to himself and to God (cf Proverbs 15:11; 16:2; 20:12; 24:12). Many times a man will cover up his true feelings with an outward show of something else: "Even in laughter the heart is sad, and the end of joy is grief" (Proverbs 14:13). Such a situation in man's

---

[31]Charles T. Fritsch, *The Interpreter's Bible*, volume 4, *Psalms, Proverbs* (Nashville, 1955), *p* 862.

nature reveals the impossibility of having a perfect fellowship among men; but such is possible with God for he knows the heart of man. In relation to this, Dächsel wrote, "Each man is a little world in himself, which God only fully sees through and understands. His sorrow appertaining to his innermost life, and his joy, another is never able fully to transfer to himself. Yea, the most sorrowful of all experiences, the most inward of all joys, we possess altogether alone, without any to participate with us."[32]

The apostle Paul urges Christians to, "Rejoice with those who rejoice, weep with those who weep" (Romans 12:15). Such kind and brotherly sympathy is a rich blessing to those who need such. Men ought to place themselves in full and complete sympathy with those in difficulty and rejoice with those who have occasions of joy. This admonition does not contradict what the Proverbs writer says about man's inability to know his fellowman's most inward feelings. While it is true that man has not the ability to know one's innermost feelings, he must involve himself with their successes and failures, for the love and concern of Christ kindles within a sensitivity to the concerns of others.

(v) Good news makes man have fat bones—"The light of the eyes rejoices the heart, the good news refreshes[33] the bones" (Proverbs 15:30). In contrast to this, "A cheerful heart is a good medicine, but a downcase spirit dries up the bones" (Proverbs 17:22). It seems that one of the godlike qualities of life ought to be that of cultivating a cheerful outlook on life and striving to be a bearer of good news to others. This is as deliberate an act as the attempt to control one's disposition, or the act of determining to be compassionate and caring toward others in need. What is more needful in our society today than individuals radiating cheerfulness? "Gladness of heart is the life of man, and the rejoicing of a man is length of days" (Ecclesiasticus 30:22). This emphasis on joy and cheerfulness is a part of Paul's teaching also: "Rejoice in the Lord always; again I will say, Rejoice" (Philippians 4:4). In all circumstances and under all conditions, cheerfulness should be the mood man is to strive for.

In this same trend of thought, the Proverb writer says, "Like cold water to a thirsty soul, so is good news from a far country"

---

[32]Quote taken from: F. Delitzsch, *op cit, p* 296.
[33]"maketh the bones fat" (KJV)—Hebrew—*dashen*—"makes fat." This is a Hebrew figure of speech for happiness.

(Proverbs 25:25). It was so difficult to receive news from distant countries in those early days, so any report from friends far away was like cold water to a thirsty soul. It restored the energies and gave new life to a sagging spirit. Many of the ancient commentators saw in this "Good news from a far country" a pronouncement of the Messiah.

(vi) Anxiety tears a man down—"Anxiety in a man's heart weighs him down, but a good word makes him glad" (Proverbs 12:25). This passage is internal antithetic parallelism in that the second line teaches the same truth as the first line by making a contrast. "Good word" in this scripture refers to an encouraging word. Our world is filled with individuals weighed down with worries and troubles. Destructive wars have left many on the brink of collapse. Dread of business failure and unemployment; anxiety over such items as food, clothing, and housing plague others. It is into such situations as these that the words of the Psalmist bring encouragement: "I have been young and am now old; yet I have not seen the righteous forsaken or his children begging bread" (Psalms 37:25).

The destructive force of anxiety is especially singled out by Jesus in the Sermon on the Mount: "Therefore do not be anxious. . . ." (Matthew 6:34; cf Matthew 6:25-34). Jesus urges individuals to trust in a God who cares and will take care of them and be concerned with their life. We have from Jesus the assurance of divine power and the immediate presence and helpfulness of the Spirit of God. We can be kept steady in life if we truly realize that God is holding on to us. Such a knowledge prompted Paul to write: "Rejoice in the Lord always . . . . have no anxiety about anything" (Philippians 4:4, 6).

Another passage relating to anxiety in Proverbs is Proverbs 18:14: "A man's spirit will endure sickness; but a broken spirit who can bear?" If man can maintain the will to live, he can endure almost anything. If the will to live is gone, however, all is lost. In this scripture, "spirit," (Hebrew—*ruach*) is the primary, sustaining principle of life which comes directly from God. The word "spirit" in the first part of this passage is masculine in gender, while in the second part "spirit" is feminine in gender. Thus, the manly spirit is represented as strong in God; the discouraged spirit is the spirit that does not draw its strength and support from God, that is, it is not casting all its cares on God (cf 1 Peter 5:7).

(vii) Man often pretends he is something that he is not—"Many a man proclaims his own loyalty, but a faithful man who can find?" (Proverbs 20:6). Which of us really lives up to what we inform people that we are? We often build up an image of ourselves. Man is the Great Pretender in relation to his own attributes, so much so that he might very well become as the Pharisee: "God, I thank thee that I am not like other men . . ." (Luke 18:11). To this attitude, Charles Kingsley addresses himself: "We are surely not sent into the world to get credit and reputations, but to speak such words as are given us to speak; to do such acts as are given us to do; not heeding much, nor expecting to know whether they have affected anything or nothing. Therefore, friends, be of good courage."[34] "Loyalty" in this verse is the Hebrew word, *chesed,* the word most closely associated with that self-sacrificing love of the New Testament, *agape.*

(2) The Characteristics of A Fool—The word "fool" (Hebrew— *kesil*) is used forty-nine times in the book of Proverbs, eighteen times in Ecclesiastes and three times elsewhere in the Old Testament. In the book of Proverbs, "fool" is defined as the opposite of "wise."[35] Those who love wisdom are to be praised; those who detest wisdom are fools. By contrast, those who find wisdom find life, whereas those who fail to search for and find wisdom find death. The "fool" in Proverbs is an individual whose trouble is spiritual. His chosen way of life is one of rejection of the truth and fear of the Lord.

The word "fool" occurs in two other Hebrew words in Proverbs, *ewil* (Proverbs 17:28), and *nabhal* (Proverbs 17:7). *Ewil* is defined as stupidity and stubborness. The fool is quarrelsome, has no sense of proportion, and is morally insolent. *Nabhal* adds the meaning of boorishness to the concept of "fool."

Prior to examining the characteristics of a fool, it might be well to determine what Jesus meant when he said, "But I say to you that every one who is angry with his brother shall be liable to judgment; whoever says, 'You fool!' shall be liable to the hell of fire" (Matthew 5:22). The Greek word *raca* ("raca"—KJV; "insults"— RSV) is from the Aramaic word *raca* which means "empty" or "vain." It is a term of contempt or reproach and is an expression

---

[34]Quoted from: M. B. Reckitt, *Faith and Society* (New York, 1932), *p* 82.

[35]For a review of what wisdom is and the characteristics of a wise man, see above, *pp* 49*ff.*

of anger to the extent of expressing words of murderous intentions. The writer follows this word with "fool" (Greek—*more*) which expresses an even more intense passion and hatred. Such an expression embodies a bitter judgement against one's spiritual state and decries him to certain destruction.

(i) The fool has asperations beyond his abilities—"A man of understanding sets his face toward wisdom, but the eyes of a fool are on the ends of the earth" (Proverbs 17:24). The thought set forth here is that a man of wisdom and understanding has his aim or goal before him at all times, whereas the fool wanders from one thing to another without keeping the important end goal before him at all times. Acting on principle is foreign to the lifestyle of a fool who acts on impulse. The foolish person is everywhere with his thoughts and strivings except where he ought to be. In contrast, the wise man properly and wisely uses what he has available to him and what opportunities he has at hand rather than reach out to what is impossible for him to attain.

If the foolish man has no real goal before himself, the wise man must have a definite goal. In relation to the Christian faith, the apostle Paul directs the wise man to a real goal: "One thing I do, forgetting what lies behind and straining forward to what lies ahead, I press on toward the goal for the prize of the upward call of God in Christ Jesus" (Philippians 3:13-14). Paul had a single aim and his every faculty was concentrated on that one object—eternal life in Christ.

(ii) The fool destroys himself and blames God—"When a man's folly brings his way to ruin, his heart rages against the Lord" (Proverbs 19:3; *cf* Lamentations 3:39; Ecclesiasticus 15:11-15; James 1:13-15). From Adam and Eve to our present generation, the alibi for succumbing to temptation is invariably, "It wasn't my fault! If God made me this way, why should I be held responsible for acting according to my nature?" In endowing man with certain appetites and desires, however, God is not tempting man to sin, for all these endowments are good and necessary to life. It is when man misdirects and misuses these desires and appetites that evil consequences ensue.

(iii) The fool makes a game out of wrong doing and thinks sin is fun—"It is like sport to a fool to do wrong, but wise conduct is pleasure to a man of understanding" (Proverbs 10:23). Just as a fool enjoys doing wrong, so a wise man enjoys right conduct, or wisdom (KJV). Johnson says, "The fool makes mirth out of mischief.

72

He takes delight in seeing the image of his restless and mischievous activity everywhere. The man of principle, on the contrary, draws his serene cheerfulness from faith in the Divine law of things—the sense that he is reconciled to it, and that the good must flow from it."[36] Wisdom here is seen as practical religion.

(iv) The fool does not think through his ideas, yet still wants to be heard—"A prudent man conceals his knowledge, but fools proclaim their folly" (Proverbs 12:23). The wise man reserves what he has to say for the proper time, place and persons. This does not mean that a man is not to give knowledge to others, but rather he is to consider the individual and the effect that such knowledge might have on him. This principle is utilized by Paul in Corinth. This apostle realized that many of the Corinthians were not spiritually mature enough to receive some of the things he desired to impart to them, therefore, he held himself in check (1 Corinthians 3:1-3; cf Hebrews 5:11—6:3).

In conjunction with the idea that a fool does not think through his ideas, Proverbs 18:2 reads, "A fool takes no pleasure in understanding, but only in expressing his opinion." In the KJV, "discover" (galah) means "to reveal," that is, a fool's heart "may reveal itself." The fool finds his highest joy in talking about himself and expressing his personal opinion. This reveals that much speaking is certainly no virtue for many times it involves nothing but idle conversation. Rabbi Akiba is reported to have said, "Silence is a fence around wisdom." For rashness of speech see also: Proverbs 10:19; 13:3, 16; 14:23; 15:2; 18:13.

(v) The fool retaliates immediately upon injury—The vexation of a fool is known at once, but the prudent man ignores insult" (Proverbs 12:16). A foolish man, when aroused to anger, has no idea of checking or controlling himself, but is quick to lash out against those who have moved him to anger. A post-biblical proverb says that a man is known by three things: his behavior in drinking, his conduct in money transactions, and his conduct under deep inward excitement.

The instruction given by Christ in relation to retaliation is, "If any one strikes you on the right cheek, turn to him the other also" (Matthew 5:39). The right that Jesus teaches us to forego is the right of retaliation. This is a hard teaching for man's tendency is to insist

---

[36]Taken from, W. J. Deane and S. T. Taylor-Taswell, op cit, p 209.

on his own rights. Yet this is the way of the fool! Instead of insisting on one's own rights, one is to yield them up. We may be abused and violated, but we are not to retaliate for such is the way of the fool. Paul, violated and abused more than any other disciple, wrote that the child of God is to overcome evil with good (Romans 12:19-21). Peter, likewise, urges Christians to follow the examples of Christ in refusing retaliation (1 Peter 2:22-24).

(vi) The fool repeats the same old sins that hurt him before—"Like a dog that returns to his vomit is a fool that repeats his folly" (Proverbs 26:11; cf 2 Peter 2:22). A fool seldom learns by experience. "Crush a fool in a martar with a pestle along with crushed grain, yet his folly will not depart from him" (Proverbs 27:22). Thus, it is easier to free wheat from its husks and impurities than to free a fool from his folly. It appears that sin becomes almost second nature to the fool so that it is next to impossible for him to turn away from it.

(3) The Education of Man—We emphasize again that the object of the book of Proverbs is to give man a practical education. These teachings are not directed to the Jewish nation as a whole, nor to any individual class, but to all individuals who may be searching for wisdom. Thus, the teachings deal with the practical problems of everyday life—with human experience in all its varied forms. Anyone who reads Proverbs is impressed with the high ethical standards of its contents. In fact, the teachings of the wise man in Proverbs has become respectably linked with the religion of Israel. With these thoughts in mind, let us examine what Proverbs has to say about the education of man.

(i) The instructors of man—Proverbs lists at least three instructors in the process of educating man—the Lord, the father, and the teacher. One who is alert to life and desires to be more than mediocre will train himself to listen to and emulate his instructors. These instructors are:

(a) The Lord—"My son, do not despise the Lord's discipline or be weary of his reproof, for the Lord reproves him whom he loves, as a father the son in whom he delights" (Proverbs 3:11-12; cf Hebrews 12:5-6). God is here viewed as the teacher who disciplines man in order to train and develop him into maturity. He seeks to punish when necessary, not to bring about destruction, but to bring about quality of character and lifestyle. F. Delitzsch translates "discipline" (musar) as "school": "The school of Jahve, my son, despise thou not . . ." for the Hebrew word, musar, means literally, "to take one into school."[37] The wise man will be taught by the Lord. It is as the Lord spoke through the prophet Isaiah, "I am the Lord your God, who teaches you to profit, who leads you in the way you should go" (Isaiah 48:17).

(b) The father—From Proverbs 4:1-4 we learn that the wise man had himself received his first instruction from his father: "When I was a son with my father, tender, the only one in the sight of my mother, he taught me . . ." (Proverbs 4:3-4). The fact of the matter is that the parent is the first teacher of any individual. Earlier the writer of Proverbs said, "Hear, my son, your father's instruction, and reject not your mother's teaching" (Proverbs 1:8). In the same manner, Moses was directed by God to impress upon the Israelites the importance of the father's primary task in the education of his children, Deuteronomy 6:6-7. The wise man, when tempted to be foolish, recalls the moral training received from his father.

Benjamin Disraeli, the famous British statesman of Jewish descent and author stated well, 'The youth of a nation are the trustees of posterity." How well we listen to our "wise" fathers will be a decisive factor in determining our future attitudes and actions in religion, in the home, and in the society. "And now, O Israel, give heed to the statutes and the ordinances which I teach you, and do them; . . . make them known to your children and your children's children" (Deuteronomy 4:1, 9). Thus, the direction and aim of instructions from the father are designed to foster wise habits of thought and action which equipt one to find his way through life with sureness (cf Proverbs 3:23; 4:12) and with honor (cf Proverbs 1:9; 4:8-9).

(c) The teacher—In referring to the words of a wise man, or a teacher, the writer of Proverbs states, "The words of a man's mouth are deep waters; the fountain of wisdom is a gushing stream" (Proverbs 18:4). In the apocryphal book of Ecclesiasticus, the writer says that his knowledge started as a trickle, then a stream, then a river, etc. There is, therefore, a great power of spiritual and moral advancement in the words of a good teacher. The writer of Proverbs assures us, "Death and life are in the power of the tongue . . ." (Proverbs 18:21). We can easily understand why the wise man is conscious of the power of speech. Words can harm or hurt, not only the person speaking them (cf James 3:1), but also

---

[37]F. Delitzsch, op cit, p 90.

the person who receives them. Thus, of supreme importance is the selection of a "wise" teacher.

(ii) The importance of education to man—"Train up a child in the way he should go, and when he is old he will not depart from it" (Proverbs 22:6). This verse expresses the importance of education to man. The Hebrews were insistent that their people be given moral training early in life when the mind is most impressionable. The result of such training will be a manner of godly living that becomes second nature. To fail in such education would be to foster attitudes in young lives that will create problems in every area of life, social and religious.

The use of the rod is encouraged as part of the educational process (cf Proverbs 13:24; 19:18; 23:13-14). The modern philosophy since World War II has been to let young men and women grow up without the use of the rod. The result is that we have reaped a sharp rise in juvenile delinquency. Firm discipline will not destroy one's capacities to have a "will of his own." The rod will not hurt budding personalities but will prove to be a stimulus to develop one into a responsible and reliable citizen of God's kingdom and God's world.

Education is important because the greatest joy that parents can have is a wise son (cf Proverbs 23:15-16, 24), while the greatest sorrow is to have a foolish son (cf Proverbs 17:21, 25). Lin Yutang writes, "The rewards of political, literary and artistic achievement produces in their authors only a pale, intellectual chuckle, while the rewards of seeing one's own children grow up big and strong are wordless and immensely real. . . . It is said that a few days before his death, Herbert Spencer had the eighteen volumes of *The Synthetic Philosophy* piled on his lap and, as he felt their cold weight, wondered if he would have done better could he have a grandchild in their stead."[38] The importance of education to man is evident—the world holds few satisfactions comparable to the growth and development of men into uprightness and integrity.

(iii) Discipline and man—The wise man knows not only how to accept reproof, but also how to administer it. "Whoever loves discipline loves knowledge, but he who hates reproof is stupid" (Proverbs 12:1; cf Proverbs 9:7-9; 15:10; 29:1). The difference between man and animals is man's ability to progress, and improve, but this capacity within man to progress is dependent upon his

---

[38]Lin Yutang, *The Importance of Living* (New York, 1937), *pp* 173-74.

willingness to accept discipline and education. Not every individual knows how to receive such correction, however. Some view rebuke as an unkind act. They interpret any correction of their personal behavior as an attempt to undermine them personally.

In disciplining or correcting another, it is imperative for one to examine his own spirit first in order to be aware that such action is not taken in a vengeful or other unChristian-like spirit. It will also be necessary to determine if the person the discipline is directed toward is mature and secure enough to profit by the action. Proper times and attitudes within the lives of those who seek to discipline can be very important in realizing success in giving direction. To discipline or correct when such is surely to be rejected will be to fail in the desired goal.

All of us will make mistakes from time to time. We are not to be despised because we do such. One who does anything in life is going to make mistakes sooner or later. The only true mistake, however, is to refuse to acknowledge a failure and to learn from such. As the inspired penman says, "He who ignores instruction despises himself, but he who heeds admonition gains understanding" (Proverbs 15:32).

The wise man, therefore, is not one who never makes mistakes, nor one who only administers reproof, but one who profits by his mistakes. He is not so much a man who gives advice as he is one who can humble himself and profit by the advice and discipline which he receives. The importance of humility is emphasized, for many times those who seem to have much less ability, experience, or intellect are in a position to advise us in life.

(iv) The importance of a receptive attitude—"The way of a fool is right in his own eyes, but a wise man listens to advice" (Proverbs 12:15). The tendency of all men is to think themselves right in all situations: "All the ways of a man are pure in his own eyes . . ." (Proverbs 16:2). Yet it is the fool who knows no other standard than his own judgment. It is the fool who continues to maintain that he always knows best in spite of warnings to the contrary. The wise man, however, is not so wise in his own eyes and is receptive to any well-intentioned counsel. Men of wisdom do not regard their own judgment as being infallible. They seek continually, from all directions, the counsel of others to help comfirm their own direction in life. Such openness of mind toward counsel cannot but lead an individual to higher and deeper wisdom.

(4) Man In His Domestic Relationships—As has been noted several

times in this study, the book of Proverbs is intensely practical. It is concerned with the daily affairs of man in this world. The practical religion taught in Proverbs is a twenty-four hour a day way of life. These things being true, we would naturally expect a book of practical injunctions, as Proverbs, to address itself to the domestic life of the man of God. We are not disappointed for Proverbs deals with every area of man's domestic life.

The importance of a proper and wholesome atmosphere in the home is obvious. The home is of such importance to the nation that we can say with certainty that the character of the home will determine the character of the nation. When the domestic relationships in the home are strong and function well, the nation will be strong and function correctly. The inverse of this is also true. The nation of Israel is a prime illustration of this truth. Every time that nation allowed its domestic life to deteriorate, the nation soon fell into decay also.

Godly homes do not come into being accidently and without effort, however. They are built and only built by dedicated and hard-working men and women who follow after the wisdom of God. The wise man faces such domestic responsibilities in a positive way for he senses something of the beauty and wonder which naturally results from a godly home-life. It is with these thoughts in mind that we turn to the book of Proverbs to examine its instructions concerning man in his domestic relationships.

There are three major areas of responsibility in the home that are emphasized in Proverbs: the husband-wife, parent-child, and master-slave relationships. If there is to be a godly home, then, each individual must fulfill his or her responsibility. Let us examine each of these individual areas of responsibility:

(i) Husband-wife relationships—The basis for a home which exhibits wisdom, strength and wholesomeness is the partnership that exists between the husband and wife. The husband and wife must work together to make the home a spiritual environment which will nurture spiritual growth. This will be no easy task. In striving to make the home what God intends for it to be, the parents must possess great persistence and patience. Such a task recalls the words of Winston Churchill when he addressed the people of Britain at the beginning of World War II: "I have nothing to offer you but blood, and sweat, and tears." If parents are to make their homes godly, they cannot but face huge tasks and obstacles. However, they are not alone for they have the assurance of God's ever-present guidance.

Much of the book of Proverbs is devoted to warnings against sexual sins. More consideration is given to this subject than any other in the book. Interestingly, the warnings are addressed entirely to men and it appears that the woman is seen as the seducer whereas the man is judged as being foolish when he goes along with the evil designs of loose women. This playing down of the guilt of man and his responsibility was probably due to the age which was one of male supremacy, for only men were given the benefit of the instruction of the wise men. While it is true that many Hebrew laws treated men and women as equals (*cf* Leviticus 20:10; 19:3; Deuteronomy 5:16; Leviticus 11; 20:11, 17-18), by and large women were considered inferior (*cf* Leviticus 12:1-5; Exodus 21:7; Leviticus 25:40; Judges 19:24). Woman's principle function was to perform as a wife and a mother.

Sex was not considered to be evil by the writer of Proverbs, nor was it to be limited to the procreation of children. The biblical view of man is that he is a creature who has biological needs and, therefore, has no reason to be ashamed of the sexual impulse. The physical relationship between husband and wife is regarded as fundamentally good. But man is also a spiritual being, created in the image of God and as a result, must guide his sexual impulses in a God-honoring manner. The fact of the matter is that the young man is exhorted to continue his sexual pleasure with the wife of his youth, who is compared to "a lovely hind" (the female of the red deer), "a graceful doe" (Proverbs 5:19).

Illicit sexual experiences were considered foolish due to the fact that they led to some very undesirable consequences, not in the moral realm so much, but in the physical, and thus the book deals with self-interest in this subject. An adulterer may lose his wealth: "And if he is caught, he will pay seven-fold; he will give all the goods of his house" (Proverbs 6:31). Disease may also result from his folly: "At the end of your life you groan, when your flesh and body are consumed" (Proverbs 5:11). Not only these things, but the man will not escape the wrath of the congregation of God's people: "I was at the point of utter ruin in the assembled congregation" (Proverbs 5:14). In short, the man who engages in sexual immorality is foolish, since he does not properly consider the serious consequences that follow such action. The whole matter can be summed up in this proverb: "He who commits adultery has no sense; he who does it destroys himself" (Proverbs 6:32).

We must not think, however, that there is no interest in Proverbs on man's morality in relation to his spiritual situation before God. Man is encouraged to avoid sexual immorality for his own physical good, but also for his spiritual welfare. In warning man against immoral women and encouraging him to be faithful to his wife, the writer says, "For a man's ways are before the eyes of the Lord, and he watches all his paths. The iniquities of the wicked ensnare him, and he is caught in the toils of his sin. He dies for lack of discipline, and because of his great folly he is lost" (Proverbs 5:21-23). The distinctive thing about the biblical conception of sex is that it fully acknowledges the reality and importance of sex as a biological function of man, but also insists that it is a function of the total personality which at its highest level is spiritual. Sex is always viewed in the Bible as a function of the whole personality, animal as well as spiritual, but the primacy of the spiritual is never forgotten.

(a) Husbands—the husband is exhorted to faithfulness to his wife in Proverbs 5:15-20. A happy and honorable marriage is the only safe-guard against the temptations of sexual immorality. The writer of Genesis says, "Therefore a man leaves his father and his mother and cleaves to his wife and they become one flesh" (Genesis 2:24). In the New Testament, the apostle Paul writes, "Husbands, love your wives, as Christ loved the church and gave himself up for her . . . . husbands should love their wives as their own bodies. He who loves his wife loves himself" (Ephesians 5:25, 28). Thus, the husband should love his wife as his own flesh and because they are two sharers in the highest and holiest things in life. To violate this holy state by sexual immorality would be to violate and degrade oneself.

In Oriental imagery the wife is described in terms of a fountain and sexual enjoyment in the terms of drinking water. A similar imagery is used by the apostles Paul and Peter as they speak of the wife as "the vessel" (1 Thessalonians 4:4; 1 Peter 3:7—KJV; the RSV uses the terms "wife" and "weaker sex" respectively for "vessel"[39]). In the same imagery, the terms "springs" and "streams of water" in Proverbs 5:16 refer to children and are an exhortation to let one's own marriage be blessed with children who may go forth and do good. The blessings from such children are in sharp

---

[39] The Greek word is *skeuos,* which means literally, "vessel."

contrast to the works of children born out of unlawful sexual relations, which children may or may not be one's own children (*cf* Proverbs 5:17).

Having emphasized the importance of the home as the foundation of the society, we realize the grave damage that can be done to a home by an unfaithful husband. Wilson writes that the unfaithful husband "has sinned against his own flesh, against the wife of another, and against the woman's husband. In a larger sense the aggressor has sinned against the community, since he has wronged a man's family and violated, whether openly or covertly, the sacredness of marriage. He has contributed to the weakening and perhaps the destruction of a home, and even if society should be so corrupt as to wink at his behavior, the moral foundations of society have been weakened."[40]

The husband is to guard himself against unfaithfulness to his wife for the good of himself, his wife, and the society. He should also be restrained by the fact that the Lord is concerned with all the ways of a man: "For a man's ways are before the eyes of the Lord, and he watches all his paths" (Proverbs 5:21). In conjunction with the duties the husband owes himself, his wife, and the community, are the duties he owes God. Being aware of God's interest and concern for his total life, man ought to be motivated toward a higher moral life.

(b) Wives—We have often been told, and even tend to believe it ourselves, that it is a man's world. But is this really true? Who gets all the attention when a child is born? when a couple gets married? when a man dies? In each case it is the woman, the bride, and the widow. One of the grandest and most thrilling roles a woman can fill is that of being a devoted wife and mother. The writer of Proverbs believes this also, for he gives responsibilities to the woman, most of which center around her domestic life.

The writer of Proverbs assures us that, "A good wife is the crown of her husband . . ." (Proverbs 12:4), but that "It is better to live in a corner of the housetop than in a house shared with a contentious woman" (Proverbs 21:9). Wives are urged not to be contentious or quarrelsome. The corner of the housetop was a small room normally reserved for guests (*cf* 2 Kings 4:10) and it would be

---

[40]Herman O. Wilson, *Studies in Proverbs* (Austin, Texas, 1969), pp. 62-63.

ironical that the master of the household should be driven there by his wife's tongue (*cf* Proverbs 21:19; 25:24).

The Arabs have a proverb that reads: "Three things render a house uninhabitable—*altakk* (rain leaking through), *alnakk* (a wife's nagging), and *albakk* (bugs)."[41] So also the writer of Proverbs: "A wife's quarreling is a continual dripping of rain" (Proverbs 19:13). A wife can be man's most satisfying delight, or a source of great misfortune.

A contentious woman is again mentioned: "A continual dripping on a rainy day and a contentious woman are alike; to restrain her is to restrain the wind or to grasp oil in his right hand" (Proverbs 27:15-16). To grasp a handful of wind or oil is an impossible task. Likewise, to restrain a contentious woman is equally impossible.

In contrast to a contentious wife, "A good wife is the crown of her husband" (Proverbs 12:4), and "He who find a good wife finds a good thing, and obtains favor from the Lord" (Proverbs 18:22). Then again, "House and wealth are inherited from fathers, but a prudent wife is from the Lord" (Proverbs 19:14). From this we realize that a fortunate outcome of the incalculable risk of marriage is taken as a mark of the Lord's favor. The Talmud says that "A good wife is a good gift; she shall be given to a man that fears God." The wife is to be the complement of the husband, and so provide for them both a rich and full life. The woman was no haphazard after-thought of the creation, but rather the crowning act, a companion suited for man.

The ideal wife and her characteristics are given in the form of an acrostic poem in which the first letter of each verse follows the order of the Hebrew alphabet in Proverbs 31:10-31: "A good wife who can find? She is far more precious than jewels. The heart of her husband trusts in her, and she will have no lack of gain. She does him good, and not harm, all the days of her life. . . . She opens her mouth with wisdom, and the teaching of kindness is on her tongue. She looks well to the ways of her household, and does not eat the bread of idleness. Her children rise up and call her blessed; her husband also, and he praises her. . . . Charm is deceitful, and beauty is vain, but a woman who fears the Lord is to be praised."

[41]F. Delitzsch, *op cit, p* 27.

82

Reading this passage in its entirety, one notices the important place the woman holds in relation to her husband. She was responsible for many economic duties, business dealings, and even management, while all the time looking out for the needs of her family and home. Her life involves the home and the community (verse 20). She is also a teacher of wisdom and kindness (verse 26).

We hear of many types of women today. There are beautiful women, career women, sophisticated women, emancipated and liberated women. It is rare, however, that one hears the term "a godly woman." In today's society, especially, there is a great need for the strength of godly women. Despite men's physical strength, they often are lacking in moral and spiritual strength. The world needs the stability, the encouragement and inspiration of godly women. We need women who will exemplify and demonstrate those special graces of womanhood which have always had their greatest sway in the home and in their own unique functions as wives and mothers of men. It was for this that women were specially and divinely created.

The duties and responsibilities of the wife and mother are great and we ought to pray for them. We pray for the rulers of the world, for church leaders, and for men in uniform. Why do we not pray more often for the wives and mothers? On their shoulders rest the responsibilities of bearing and nurturing our children. They determine the atmosphere of our homes, the conscience and character of our children, and the destiny of our nation. Napoleon once asked of Madam Campana, "What is wanting in order that the youth of France will be well educated?" Her reply was, "Good mothers." Surely the old proverb is true: "The hand that rocks the cradle, rules the world."

(ii) Parent-child relationships—Once again the emphasis in Proverbs on guidance and discipline will come to the forefront as the writer deals with the parent-child relationship. "The rod and reproof give wisdom, but a child left to himself brings shame to his mother" (Proverbs 29:15). In contrast to this, a disciplined child will bring happiness to his mother: "Discipline your son, and he will give your rest; he will give delight to your heart" (Proverbs 29:17). The mentioning of the mother, and not the father, in this passage may be due to the mother's tender love which often degenerates into fond indulgence. The phrase "left to himself."[42] is

---

[42]Hebrew—*meshalach*—"being free to roam."

used of animals pasturing at liberty, wandering in freedom (*cf* Job 39:5; Isaiah 16:2). God holds the parents responsible for disciplining their children, and contrary to popular opinion, most children want guidelines established and disciplined used by their parents. Children have impulses and urges that need to be directed and trained.

Another great lesson in the parent-child relationship set forth by Proverbs is that the parents who refuse to discipline their children in reality act as if they despise them: "He who spares the rod hates his son, but he who loves him is diligent to discipline him" (Proverbs 13:24). And again, "Discipline your son while there is hope; do not set your heart on his destruction" (Proverbs 19:18). As God disciplines those whom he loves (*cf* Proverbs 3:12), so parents discipline children they love.

In disciplining, however, it is imperative that the parents take care to let their children know and feel that all such measures of correction are done with a deep and pervading parental love. Such love seeks the highest welfare of the one loved. In the New Testament, Hebrews 12:5-11 draws attention to the imperfect motives of human fathers, and Ephesians 6:4 warns against undue severity. Thus, parental discipline must be meted out as God measures it out, that is, not with a harshness or unfairness, which arouses anger or resentment, but with a proper and godly spirit appropriate to followers of the Lord God.

In relation to discipline, the inspired penman says that it is actually a gift to a child: "Do not withhold discipline from a child; if you beat him with a rod, he will not die. If you beat him with a rod you will save his life from Sheol" (Proverbs 23:13-14).[43] The bitter medicine of discipline is not death producing, but rather life producing. Disciplining a child prevents him from falling into the passions of the world which lead men to death and destruction. The proper training and directing of the impulses and urges in the life of a child will produce a wholeness of life, not death, for that child. If parents do not discipline their children, they foster attitudes within them that will lead the children to trouble with the laws of the land and the laws of God. To be cheated of such

---

[43]"Life" *(naphash)* in the scriptures very often means simply, "physical life," and Sheol *(sheol)* means "death" or "the grave." Thus, verse 13 is speaking of physical death, and its parallel, verse 14, refers to physical death, or the grave.

instruction, with all the discipline and even punishment necessarily involved, can produce a child with a life-long anger.

The parent-child relationship in Proverbs also emphasizes the responsibilities of the children in various areas. A child must develop a deep appreciation for parents who discipline: "Hearken to your father who begot you, and do not despise your mother when she is old" (Proverbs 23:22). To "hearken" is equivalent to obeying. The New Testament, in harmony with this advice, teaches: "Children, obey your parents in the Lord, for this is right. 'Honor your father and mother' (this is the first commandment with a promise), 'that it may be well with you and that you may live long on the earth' " (Ephesians 6:1-3). Young people face the great temptation of trying to make themselves lord of their lives in the home and thus defy their parents. In contrast to such an attitude, a child that is properly disciplined will not be a worry and concern to his parents in later years.

The responsibilities of children to their *aged* parents who are dependent upon them is also addressed in Proverbs: "He who does violence to his father and chases away his mother is a son who causes shame and brings reproach" (Proverbs 19:26). Consideration for parents is regarded as both a mark of the wise and a motive for wisdom. On the other hand, there is some very strong language against those who do not honor their parents: "If one curses his father or his mother, his lamp will be put out in utter darkness" (Proverbs 20:20). The inner man is the lamp that is put out, which means that a failure to achieve inner peace and happiness is the result. Children owe their aged parents honor, love, respect, care and financial aid if needed. The divinely revealed responsibilities to love and respect parents is a lifetime requirement.

The warning against disregard and disrespect for parents is continued in Proverbs 30:17: "The eye that mocks a father and scorns to obey a mother will be picked out by the ravens of the valley and eaten by the vultures." Such a disregard for parents has always been considered a grave offense by the writers of God's word. It has been considered punishable by death (*cf* Exodus 21:17; Leviticus 20:9; Deuteronomy 27:16; Matthew 15:4). There are many good as well as bad things abroad in the world and the work of good parents is to see that their children do not become victims of the evil and false influences to which they are subject as they pursue the good things of the world. As much of the good should be sought as will better fit the child for godly service. Longfellow's,

"The Chamber Over the Gate," voices a well-known and poignant reminder of the pain that results from a wayward child:

"It is so far from thee
Thou canst no longer see,
In the chamber over the Gate,
That old man desolate,
Weeping and wailing sore
For his son, who is no more?
 O Absalom, my son!"

In contrast to the foolish son who does not harken to his parents, and the resulting family shame, is the joy which a wise son bestows: "A wise son hears his father's instruction, but a scoffer does not listen to rebuke" (Proverbs 13:1). The emphasis throughout Proverbs on the intellectual recognition of the right as the basis of the good life is allied to the conception that if one knows what is right, he will do what is right.

Today's homes face many complex problems. The only wise solution to these complex problems is to enthrone God in the heart and life of every family member. The pat answers and simple solutions given in the past are no solutions. Today's problems are too complex. It takes hard work, long hours and many other ingredients to make a spiritually sound and healthy home. We cannot expect a better world without better homes, and we cannot expect better homes without better parents.

(iii) Master-slave relationships—Old Testament Palestine was economically and socially an integral part of the ancient Near Eastern world. Slavery was an economic institution and, as a result, Palestine had slave systems like its neighbors. The economy of Palestine was based on free labor. The activities of the slave, however, centered mostly in the household of the rich, and the slave was primarily a domestic servant rather than an agricultural or industrial worker. With these thoughts in mind we turn to the master-slave relationships as discussed in the book of Proverbs.

The first thing of note is that the master always is to treat his servant in such a way that the servant recognizes his position of subjection: "By mere words a servant is not disciplined, for though he understands, he will not give heed. . . . He who pampers his servant from childhood, will in the end find him his heir" (Proverbs 29:19, 21; cf Ecclesiasticus 33:24-28). It is necessary to provide firm and just government to those who serve in order that they might remain in grateful service and not rebel in ingratitude. A servant pampered will forget his duties and responsibilities and try to assume the rights and privileges of his master.

The master is also warned against elevating a slave to a position of prominence above others: "It is not fitting for a fool to live in luxury, much less for a slave to rule over princes" (Proverbs 19:10). It was a common practice for Eastern monarchs at times to place a favorite slave over the very princes and nobles of the land. Ecclesiastes speaks of this: "I have seen slaves on horses, and princes walking on foot like slaves" (Ecclesiastes 10:7). A person who was once a slave and has attained position and wealth often becomes a tyrant. It would be poor judgment to take men who have had the opportunity and training for positions of leadership and prominence and replace them with those of no reputation, training or character.

Slaves did have certain rights and privileges, however. One of these was the right to protection against false accusations: "Do not slander a servant to his master, lest he curse you, and you be held guilty" (Proverbs 30:10). Interference in the affairs of another man's household was forbidden. One is not to bring a charge against a man's slave and make his master suspicious of him. The position of a slave, at best, is not good, thus the exhortation not to make a slave's situation in life worse by false accusations.

A slave could also take part in the inheritance of his master. In normal situations the property of the master was divided among his sons, the elder son receiving a double share (Deuteronomy 21:15-17). If there were no sons, the daughter, or daughters, might inherit the property, but not the wife. If a man died with no children, the property would go to his male next of kin (Numbers 27:8-11), or to an adopted son who might be a former slave (Genesis 15:2-3). The precise situation set forth in Proverbs 17:2, where a slave takes the share of a renegade son, is not provided for in the Mosaic Law: "A slave who deals wisely will rule over a son who acts shamefully, and will share the inheritance as one of the brothers" (Proverbs 17:2). Abraham's servant, Eliezer of Damascus, was at one time considered the patriarch's heir (Genesis 15:2-3). Ziba, Saul's servant, obtained the inheritance of his lord Mephibosheth (2 Samuel 16:4; *cf* 1 Chronicles 2:34; Ecclesiasticus 10:25). The Proverb writer probably is alluding to the possibility that a careful and wise servant may rise to a position of prominence in the household (as did Joseph in Egypt), and especially if the sons of the master were not what they should have been. This proverb was strikingly borne out in the situation with Solomon's servant and son (1 Kings 11:26*ff*).

(5) Man In His Social Relationships—Proverbs gives man some good advice on how to live in the social world. One might live with the world of nature with some measure of appreciation and understanding. He might even have achieved the ability to live at peace with himself, but if he has not learned how to get along with other people, he has still to accomplish one of the most important tasks in life. This task is important for there is no individual growth apart from one's social relationships. Every individual develops and grows due to the direction and influence he derives from those within his social environment.

Several years ago, the University of Chicago and the American Association for adult education conducted a survey to determine what adults wanted to study above all things. This survey took two years and cost $25,000. It revealed that the subject of how to understand and get along with people—how to make people like you—is of greater interest to adults than any other subject, with the single exception of personal health. Dale Carnegie and his courses, founded in 1912, have organized themselves around this need. Today this is a world-wide institution which has proven itself valuable in the social and business world. The book of Proverbs is an inspired work of God which also reveals to man how he can get along with and influence people in his social relationships.

(i) Social calls—"Let your foot be seldom⁴⁴ in your neighbor's house, lest he become weary of you and hate you" (Proverbs 25:17). In other words, we should not make too many visits to our neighbor's house in order that we do not wear out our welcome. It would be better that the visits be few and far between than frequent and wearisome. A German proverb reads, "Let him who seeks to be of esteem come seldom." A person who does not wear out his welcome has a foot that is "made precious" or "made prized" by its infrequent visits. There must always be moderation and consideration for other people's feelings and convenience.

(ii) Friendship—Men are to strive to be genuine friends and not take their friends for granted. Like love, friendship calls for the treatment of others as subjects of intrinsic worth rather than as

---

⁴⁴Hebrew—*yaqar*—"make rare" or "make precious."

objects of instrumental value. Changes of weather and times of adversity do not change the devotion and loyalty of a true friend. On the contrary, such times and changes only deepen the friendship. This is because friendship is not a method of using people to further one's own goals and ambitions, rather it is a way of appreciating them and respecting them for what they are.

The writer of Proverbs exhorts: "Your friend and your father's friend, do not forsake; and do not go to your brother's house in the day of calamity" (Proverbs 27:10). One of the greatest gifts a man might have is the kind of love involved in genuine friendship. Such a gift must be nurtured, cared for, and protected. Thus the emphasis on not forsaking friends of oneself or of the family. The possession of friends is truly a prize of great value.

The above proverb (27:10) also teaches that in time of calamity one should not take the attitude that help and assistance are deserving and should necessarily be forthcoming from others, including one's own family. To receive help from friends in times of calamity is to be a cause of great joy and such ought to be gratefully appreciated and received. Many times such assistance comes from friends even before one's own blood brother. And such help is given by those who love and not because it is demanded and must be given. The old attitude that expresses itself in the phrase, "You owe me!" is false.

In addressing the topic of friendship, Proverbs 27:10c continues: "Better is a neighbor who is near than a brother who is far away." A neighbor who is helpful is of far greater value than a brother who, though close blood-wise, is not concerned with the affairs of his relation. Unless a blood relationship is founded on a deep sharing and upon more than the accident of birth, it cannot have the depth of quality that a real friendship has. Jesus pointed out that there were ties stronger than family ties when he said, "For whoever does the will of my Father in heaven is my brother, and sister, and mother" (Matthew 12:50; cf Matthew 10:34-37).

Some friends are easily made, but unless such friendships are built on a solid foundation, they are just as easily broken: "There are friends who pretend to be friends, but there is a friend who sticks closer than a brother" (Proverbs 18:24). Superficial friends are easily gained and lost, but true friends are for a lifetime. True friends spend time together and need and enjoy each other's company. Thus, a multitude of friends is not necessarily a good thing. Friendship is not a thing of quantity, but of quality.

In describing the durability of true friendship, the writer of Proverbs points out, "A friend loves at all times, and a brother is born for adversity" (Proverbs 17:17). One of the greatest tests of true friendship is adversity, and to have a friend in times of adversity is to possess a precious gift. True friendship is based on constancy, or loyalty, a loyalty that expresses itself is faithfulness. As Wilson has pointed out:

> Every normal person . . . seeks approbation or consolation from a small circle of friends. One's friends make a victory or achievement sweeter by acclaiming it, and they reduce the pain of disappointment or defeat by sharing it. In our friends we find our favorable characteristics approved and our confidence strengthened; in their kindness we find our weak and less noble qualities minimized and softened. Thus in moments of exultation or in time of need we turn to our friends—and are not disappointed.[45]

Robert Lewis Stevenson points out the value of friends when he writes, "So long as we are loved by others, I would almost say that we are indispensable; and no man is useless while he has a friend."[46] In this same line of thinking, John MacCunn writes, "Once any man has true friends, he never again frames his decisions, even those which are most secret, as if he were alone in the world. He frames them habitually in the imagined company of his friends. In their visionary presence he thinks and acts; and by them, as visionary tribunal, he feels himself, even in his unspoken intentions and inmost feelings, to be judged."[47]

One of life's greatest blows is to have a friend taken away by death. Yet, at the same time, the value of friendship is such that not even death can destroy it. Seneca, first century Roman poet and later tutor to Nero, in seeking to comfort Marullus, offered this assurance: "The comfort of having a friend may be taken away, but not that of having had one. It is an ill construction of providence to reflect only upon my friend's being taken away, without any regard to the benefit of his once being given to me. He that has lost a friend has more cause of joy that once he had him, than of grief that he is taken away."[48]

---

[45]Herman O. Wilson, *op cit, p* 15.

[46]Robert Lewis Stevenson, *Lay Morals and Other Papers* (New York, 1911), *p* 50.

[47]John MacCunn, *The Making of Character* (New York, 1900), *p* 93.

[48]*Moral Epistles*, XCIX.

Caution is to be used in the selection of friends: "Make no friendship with a man given to anger, nor go to a wrathful man, lest you learn his ways and entangle yourself in a snare" (Proverbs 22:24-25). This is essentially the same advice given to Christians by the apostle Paul in his letter to Corinth: "Do not be deceived: 'Bad company ruins good morals' " (1 Corinthians 15:33). It is the man of wisdom who avoids those who have characteristics which are not worthy of the man of God. In our society we cannot escape the moral and psychological consequences of the fact that we are members one of another. It is imperative, therefore, that we carefully choose our friends for the influence of our companions affect us in every way. In speaking of humanity, John Donne, the seventeenth century poet, said what holds true of our moral situation also: "No man is an *Islande,* intire of it selfe; every man is a peece of the *Continent,* a part of the *maine;* . . . any man's *death* diminishes *me,* because I am involved in *Mankinde;* And therefore never send to know for whom the *bell* tolls; it tolls for *thee.*"[49]

A real friend is most concerned with his friend's best interest and not in preserving the friendship for the sake of the friendship. "Better is open rebuke than hidden love. Faithful are the wounds of a friend, profuse are the kisses of an enemy" (Proverbs 27:5-6). "Hidden love" is a love which does not make itself known in some outward act of rebuke or correction, which is no real love at all. The "faithful wounds of a friend" means that a true friend's love is not weak sentimentality but rather it involves an unselfish criticism. True friends consider the welfare of another and point out the friend's mistakes or other dangers to the development of a godly character (Ephesians 4:15). Such is painful and difficult to do, but to put forth false praise is to fail in true friendship. Gregory I is reported to have said, "I think that man is my friend through whose advice I am enabled to wipe off the blemishes of my soul before the appearance of the awful Judge." The "kisses of an enemy" carry one's thoughts back to the false friendship of Judas who lavished kisses upon Jesus of Nazareth the night of betrayal.

Finally, in relation to friends, the writer of Proverbs assures his readers that a friend makes his companions better people: "Iron

---

[49] John Donne, *Devotions, ed* John Sparrow (London, 1923), *p* 92.

sharpens iron, and one man sharpens another" (Proverbs 27:17). As iron is sharpened by iron, so man sharpens the appearance, deportation, nature and character of his friends. The wise man, therefore, associates with those individuals that sharpen him morally and spiritually.

(iii) The rich and the poor—As did the eighth century prophets, the writer of Proverbs reveals a great interest in the treatment and welfare of the poor. A constant emphasis in the wisdom teachings is, "To do righteousness and justice is more acceptable to the Lord than sacrifice" (Proverbs 21:3). In spite of this emphasis, however, it was so difficult for men of wealth to keep the proper perspective in their dealings with the poor. There was the continual danger that wealth tends to make one callous and insensitive to the needs of those poor near him. It is due to this unbalance that the book of Proverbs is strong in its condemnation against the rich who oppress the poor.

God promises to bless the labor of the righteous poor: "The fallow ground of the poor yields much food, but it is swept away through injustice" (Proverbs 13:23). While this passage is very difficult in the Hebrew text, the usual interpretation is that while the new land of a poor man produces a great crop due to his labor and the blessings of God, the land of the rich man fails due to his unjust actions. Delitzsch writes: "While the (Industrious and God-fearing) poor man is richly nourished from the piece of ground which he cultivates, many a one who has incomparably more than he comes by his unrighteousness down to a state of beggary, or even lower: he is not only in poverty, but along with this his honour, his freedom, and the very life of his person perish."[50]

Proverbs teaches that a poor man does not have friends because he is of no advantage to people: "All a poor man's brothers hate him; how much more do his friends go far from him" (Proverbs 19:7). The Hebrew word for "hate" (sane) does not mean to hate in the sense of despising, but rather it means to be unconcerned for, the absence of positive, active concern. It refers to attitudes and actions rather than emotions. Because the poor have so little to offer, it is so easy to disregard them, to pass by on the other side.

The apostle John expresses this same concern for the poor when he writes, "But if anyone has the world's goods and sees his brother

---

[50]Delitzsch, op cit, p 286.

in need, yet closes his heart against him, how does God's love abide in him?" (1 John 3:17). To disregard those in need is impossible unless the love of God is not given its proper place in the individual's heart. One's love for God is given its proper meaning and manifestation in a life only as it is expressed in one's relationship with others. Love is practical and requires doing the little things and making the day to day petty sacrifices which few notice or applaud.

To receive help from God of necessity includes helping the poor: "He who closes his ear to the cry of the poor will himself cry out and not be heard" (Proverbs 21:13). This teaching is in principle like the teaching of Jesus when he emphasized that his followers should not ask for forgiveness unless they have first forgiven their fellowmen (Matthew 6:14-15). God's divine assistance is linked with man's assistance to others. This truth is vividly expressed in the parable of the Rich Man and Lazarus (Luke 16:19-31). While on earth the rich man had ample opportunity to assist Lazarus, the begger, but he did not. When it was too late; when the rich man needed God's help; he wished then that all were different; he wished that he had been concerned with helping the poor (cf the judgment scene of Matthew 25:31-46).

In contrast with neglecting the poor, if we help the poor God will help us: "He who is kind to the poor lends to the Lord, and he will repay him for his deed" (Proverbs 19:17). The wise man teaches that proper care should be taken of the poor, just as the prophets later taught (cf Amos 2:6-7; 4:1; 5:15; Isaiah 10:1-2; etc). This is not just a passive admonition either, but rather an exhortation to take active measures to aid the poor. When one is kind to the poor, he is in reality kind to God. Again, it is possible to neither despise nor pity a man, yet hate him by being indifferent towards him by merely tolerating or ignoring him. The priest and the Levite in the parable of the Good Samaritan (Luke 10:30-37) were not aggressively evil toward the traveler, nor were they positively compassionate; they were indifferent. This attitude is contrasted by the wise man who says, "He who despises his neighbor is a sinner, but happy is he who is kind to the poor" (Proverbs 14:21).

In another proverb we are assured, "He who gives to the poor will not want, but he who hides his eyes will get many a curse" (Proverbs 28:27).[51] And in parallel with this, "He who oppresses

---

[51]This phrase, "he who hides his eyes," means to turn one's eye that he may not see the poor, or to pretend not to notice the poor.

the poor . . . will only come to want" (Proverbs 22:16). It takes great faith to believe the truth of these proverbs, that is, the fact that greed is self-defeating. We are, nonetheless, assured that God will, in some manner, compensate for what is spent on the poor, by shedding his blessings on the giver. In contrast, those who oppress the poor for self-gain will fail in the end.

᛫ Finally, in relation to the poor, the Proverb writer assures his readers that the poor are as much a part of God's creation as the rich, and must be treated as such: "He who oppresses a poor man insults his Maker, but he who is kind to the needy honors him" (Proverbs 14:31). "Insults his Maker," means that one thinks God is not wise for placing the poor on earth. The poor, however, have a place in God's world and plan. Jesus even taught, "For you always have the poor with you" (Matthew 26:11). Jesus also places the duty of caring for the poor on the high ground of his solidarity with his people: "As you did it to one of the least of these my brethren, you did it to me" (Matthew 25:40). Therefore, to harrass and oppress the poor due to their lowly state is an offense against God. The poor and the rich all share alike in their common relationship to God as Creator.

(6) Man In His Economic Relationships—Since Proverbs has a basic concern for man and his practical life, it naturally follows that it has a concern for the economic order of the society. It would certainly be an unhappy state of affairs if God were not interested in the economic situation of man. The fact of the matter is, however, that God does have this concern and he gives special instructions on how to live in an economic world such as we have today. The book of Proverbs is concerned with religious and moral questions, but it is equally concerned with economic issues and how men of God can and should confront such issues in their day to day living.

(i) Rules for different occupations—In an ode that appears to be in praise of the pastoral and agricultural lifestyles, the wise man encourages his readers to avoid the temptations of investing all one's time and energy in the things that do not endure, such as politics and the seeking of worldly prominence and wealth, Proverbs 27:23-27. History bears out well the transciency of governments, prosperity and prominence. The wise man will not devote his energies toward the mad scramble for money and position. This does not mean that the only way of life is the pastoral or agricultural, but rather that there is grave danger of placing life's importance in the business world which is not as enduring as the pastoral and agricultural aspects of life. The wise man will keep a healthy balance in his thinking and occupations by a continual recognition of the purposes and sufficiency of God. The things of value in this world can be acquired, not by reliance on the powers of the world, but upon self-diligence in one's activities, coupled with a trust in God to give the increase.

(ii) Labor and laziness—Competence in one's trade or profession entails a special kind of "wisdom," according to the wise man: "Do you see a man skillful in his work? he will stand before kings; he will not stand before obscure men" (Proverbs 22:29). It is imperative that an individual be diligent in his work, and the reward for such diligence is that he will stand before kings and work for them rather than remain in the obscure work of the average man. The lazy man is an ordinary man whose life and contribution to the world are also average or ordinary. The lazy man's life is without real meaning for it is a life of making excuses, postponing tasks, and refusing opportunities. God created each and every individual with a plan in mind, and that plan is to use one's abilities and talents in such a manner that the Creator is honored and the neighbor is assisted or benefited. To fail to give the world the products of one's life is to be foolish and ungodly.

"A slothful man will not catch his prey, but the diligent man will get precious wealth" (Proverbs 12:27). The man of diligence will be provided the necessities of life, whereas the lazy man is so indolent that he cannot even get his own food (cf Proverbs 12:27; 19:24). The lazy man falls into hunger when the time of want comes for he has not worked in preparation for the lean days of the year. He has failed to realize that the accumulation of food is not the result of man's wishes, but of man's diligence. The result of such a failure to provide for oneself is that the community has the responsibility of providing for itself and sharing of its proceeds with the sluggard. The burden of work is made heavier on others by the one who is lazy. In such a situation, the words of the apostle Paul are valuable: "If any one will not work, let him not eat" (2 Thessalonians 3:10).

In fighting against those who would encourage him to work, the lazy man can be very ingenuious in devising the most improbable alarms. He convinces himself that there are always great obstacles in the way preventing him from working. The sluggard says, "There is a lion outside! I shall be slain in the streets" (Proverbs 22:13).

The point of this satire is to show the preposterous excuses offered by the lazy. How exasperating it must be to those who must employ the lazy. If you want a thing done well and promptly, however, never select a person with plenty of leisure time. Employ the busiest person you can find. All the really worthwhile things in life are done by busy men and women. The excuse-giver always obeys the lower voice and leaves unfulfilled the will of God.

The lazy and indolent individual is referred to again by the writer of Proverbs in Proverbs 26:13-16:

"The sluggard says, 'There is a lion in the road!
There is a lion in the streets!'
As a door turns on its hinges,
so does a sluggard on his bed.
The sluggard buries his hand in the dish;
it wears him out to bring it back to his mouth.
The sluggard is wiser in his own eyes
than seven men who can answer discreetly."

Again, the inspired writer refers to the excuses offered by the lazy person such as the danger of lions in the streets. The writer then likens the sluggard to a gate which never moves anywhere, it merely turns on its hinges going nowhere. So, in like manner, the lazy man turns on his bed, always ready to give some pretext for evading work. The lazy man is even too lazy to raise his hand to his mouth to eat (verse 15), or to raise his arm to ask a question in order to learn something (verse 16), for he believes that he has already acquired all knowledge. He believes himself to be wiser than seven of the wisest.

Laziness can become such a habit that one day the sluggard will wake up and realize that he has accomplished nothing: "Slothfulness casts into a deep sleep, and an idle person will suffer hunger" (Proverbs 19:15). By too many excuses, refusals and postponements, the sluggard will suddenly wake to find that poverty has arrived. His friends in life have gone to rewarding jobs and places in life while the sluggard's life has ended in disorder. We are reminded again of the words: "If any one will not work, let him not eat."

To the lazy man the wise man cries out: "Go to the ant, O sluggard; consider her ways, and be wise" (Proverbs 6:6). The challenge to the lazy fellow is to redeem the time and take advantage of every moment as does the ant which needs no overseer and no prodding (cf Proverbs 6:7-11). The ant works to prepare for future days and seasons. The ant is aware of the time and moves ahead in an industrious manner. Thus, the wise man is not entrapped by "a little sleep, a little slumber, a little folding of the hands." Rather he is planting, cultivating, or doing other worthwhile and useful work in preparation for future periods of leanness.

(iii) Poverty and the causes of it—We have remarked previously that Jesus taught that the poor would always be with us (Matthew 26:11). The truthfulness of this statement is evident in every age and behind such poverty are several factors. The very frequence and regularity of poverty can so easily dull the edge of our compassion. It is imperative, therefore, that we strive to discover some of the factors behind poverty, recognizing all the while the danger of oversimplification. What does the writer of Proverbs have to say about the causes of poverty?

(a) Excessiveness in food and drink—"Be not among the wine-bibbers, or among gluttonous eaters of meat; for the drunkard and the glutton will come to poverty" (Proverbs 23:20-21; cf Proverbs 23:29-35). This combination of gluttons and winebibbers was used as a reproach against Jesus (Matthew 11:19). It is hoped by the Proverb writer that, by painting the unhappy results of excessiveness, he might motivate individuals to moderation. Self-indulgence, motivated by the selfish desire to gratify one's own appetite, leads to the destruction of the body and mind, thus eventually to poverty and death. To combat this, one must regulate his conduct by principle and judgment, not impulse, desire or social custom.

(b) Following worthless pursuits—"He who tills his land will have plenty of bread, but he who follows worthless pursuits[52] will have plenty of poverty" (Proverbs 28:19; 12:11). Here is a situation in which a person does not lack industry, he lacks instead discrimination. There are so many get-rich quick schemes around to lead astray the man who is undiscerning. It is here that the ability to achieve a clear perception of the truly important activities must come into play. The problem involves the necessity of understanding coupled with the ability to give first place to the really important things and claims in life.

(c) Ignoring instructions—Many times, individuals fail in their business pursuits simply because they refuse to listen to sound

---

[52]"Worthless pursuits" (RSV), or "vain persons" (KJV)—either is possible, but "worthless pursuits" is more probable.

advice. The Proverb writer exhorts: "Poverty and disgrace come to him who ignores instruction, but he who heeds reproof is honored" (Proverbs 13:18). Great kings and leaders always have a council of advisors in their courts and places of business in order to continually benefit from their advice. To be hardened against such advice and counsel is to avoid great profit and thus open the way to poverty and disgrace.

(d) Laziness—The accumulated wealth of most individuals is not the result of their wishes and that alone, but of their diligence and hard work. The wise man seeks several opportunities to emphasize that every individual within the society must work to supply the needs and wants of mankind, Proverbs 6:6-11; 24:30-34 (cf preceeding pages). To fail to work is to rob the society of the products of one's hands and talents. To fail to work will also end in poverty and disgrace.

(iv) Wealth—The subject of wealth is frequently discussed in Proverbs. The primary emphasis is that there are many dangers involved with wealth. Riches are insecure in themselves and ill-gotten wealth is destructive to its owner. Wealth tends to make men neglect the ideal life for one not so ideal. When men have their cares and concerns for wealth, it chokes out their concern for the mind and the heart; it deadens their concern for other people's needs. In the mad scramble to secure themselves, men forget the love they owe their fellowman. A life of luxury and pleasure tends to make one callous and indifferent to the needs of those near him. But worst of all, man forgets his whole self and so stands naked before God in the midst of all his riches. The things of real value, according to the writer of Proverbs, are one's spiritual and moral treasures. The best situation in life is to be neither rich nor poor, but to have sufficient goods to satisfy the bodily good and to have good spiritual and moral treasures. What does the book of Proverbs have to say in relation to wealth?

(a) A righteous man is promised wealth—"In the house of the righteous there is much treasure, but trouble befalls the income of the wicked" (Proverbs 15:6). "The reward for humility and fear of the Lord is riches and honor and life" (Proverbs 22:4). The wise man teaches that a life devoted to God is commendable due to the rewards which it brings. Both the quantity and quality of life is to be enhanced for him who is righteous. The best things in life come to those who live in harmony with the will of God.

The popular proverb that says, "The good prosper, the evil

suffer," must not be pressed too far, however. The difficulty comes when life's experiences fail to validate this promise. Whenever a man is prosperous, this would seem to imply that he is a good man. A person who is poor or suffering might condemn himself, as well as be condemned, as a great sinner. It is obvious that the philosophy that teaches that God always punishes the wicked and gives prosperity to the good does not hold true in all situations. Did Christ suffer and die on the cross because he was an evil man? If a man loses his home in a fire, does that mean that he is a greater sinner than his neighbor who did not suffer such a tragedy? Did Job suffer because he was an unrighteous man? The answer to all these questions is obvious. Suffering is a part of life and it befalls all mankind, good or evil. No man can escape suffering. The important thing is how man responds to suffering. A righteous man, whose dependence is upon God, is far better enabled to endure suffering when it comes and as a result of it can grow and develop (cf Luke 13:1-5).

In speaking of wealth and the teachings of Proverbs on this subject, a deeper incentive than self-interest must be at work if true righteousness is achieved. A life of righteousness is rewarding, but if we strive for righteousness for the sole motive of riches and rewards, we miss the true meaning of godly wisdom and righteousness. This brings up several questions as to why man serves God. Is it for what he can get out of it? Is man capable of disinterested goodness? Is there any man who loves God without a calculating love? John 3:16 points out that God so loved that he gave. Neither is this a calculating love for when God sent his Son he had no guarantee that any one would accept him. This is a love and faith that the man of God must develop, a love and faith that exists when there may be reason not to have such.

(b) Wealth comes slowly and not quickly—"Wealth hastily gotten will dwindle, but he who gathers little by little will increase it" (Proverbs 13:11). "An inheritance gotten hastily in the beginning will in the end not be blessed" (Proverbs 20:21). "A faithful man will abound with blessings, but he who hastens to be rich will not go unpunished. . . . A miserly man hastens after wealth, and does not know that want will come upon him" (Proverbs 28:20, 22). Hastening to get rich will normally involve wrong motives and even actions on the part of the one seeking wealth. The covetous man sees only the value of gold and measures all things by that standard. The result of such values and standards is that morality and concern for the good of others is often set aside in the hasty pursuit of wealth. These verses in Proverbs place strong emphasis on diligence and industry in acquiring goods rather than seeking easy and fast methods. Few things are as perishing and short-termed as wealth. In the words of Jesus, "Seek first his (God's) kingdom and his righteousness, and all these things shall be yours as well" (Matthew 6:33).

(c) Righteousness is more important than wealth—"A good name is to be chosen rather than great riches, and favor is better than silver or gold" (Proverbs 22:1). "Better is a poor man who walks in his integrity than a rich man who is perverse in his ways" (Proverbs 28:6). In regards to a good name, Pirke Aboth 4:7 reads, "There are three crowns, the crown of the Torah, the crown of the priesthood, and the crown of the kingship, but the crown of a good name excels them all."[53] A man's real asset, then, lies not in wealth but in character. Money can bring some good into other people's lives, but not the real good that can be brought into lives by a good man who has a righteous concern for others. The moral power of a righteous man is far superior to the power of wealth. Then too, moral power is readily available to all, whereas wealth is not. Jesus gave his disciples great power but told them to count all this as little in comparison to having their names written in heaven: "Behold I have given you authority to tread upon serpents and scorpions, and over all the power of the enemy; and nothing shall hurt you. Nevertheless, do not rejoice in this, that the spirits are subject to you; but rejoice that your names are written in heaven" (Luke 10:19-20). As the apocrypha character Tobit reportedly said to his son, "And fear not, my son, that we are made poor; for thou hast much wealth, if thou fear God, and depart from all sin, and do that which is pleasing in his sight" (Tobit 4:21).

(d) A trust in riches will lead to calamity—"He who trusts in his riches will wither, but the righteous will flourish like a green leaf" (Proverbs 11:28). Individuals who trust in riches begin to depend on wealth to the extent that they live as though wealth might accomplish all that they desire to accomplish and gain them all that they desire to gain. Thus the man who trusts and depends on riches, while

---

[53]A collection of maxims, mostly ethical and religious, taught by Jewish teachers within a period extending from the third century B.C. to the third century A.D. They are also called "Sayings of the Fathers."

feeling secure, is well on his way to destruction. The main good in life, therefore, is to be found in righteousness, not in riches.

The man who trusts in riches will also devote his total efforts to acquire wealth, therefore the wise man warns: "Do not toil to acquire wealth; be wise enough to desist. When your eyes light upon it, it is gone; for suddenly it takes to itself wings, flying like an eagle towards heaven" (Proverbs 23:4-5). Riches are transitory, therefore, men are urged to be diligent and watchful in maintaining what they have and also not to trust too highly in their wealth. As Jesus taught, "How hard it is for them that trust in riches to enter the kingdom of God" (Mark 10:24, *KJV*). This is true for it is so difficult to engage in the pursuit of wealth without being in the constant temptation to close the heart to generosity, love and justice.

(e) There is a temptation to forsake God in riches and in poverty. "Two things I ask of thee; deny them not to me before I die: Remove far from me falsehood and lying; give me neither poverty nor riches; feed me with the food that is needful for me, lest I be full, and deny thee, and say, 'Who is the Lord?' or lest I be poor, and steal, and profane the name of my God" (Proverbs 30:7-9). Riches have the ability to create an artificial sense of self-importance to the extent that they may destroy religious humility and the sense of need for God. Lack of money, on the other hand, can cause one to disregard God's will and one's fellowman in attempts to get for self the good and needful things in life. Izzac Walton quoted a wise man who said, "There be as many miseries beyond riches as on this side of them."[54] More important than wealth or lack of wealth is a life of righteousness.

In relation to wealth, the Proverbs writer desires that every man work and live on the proceeds of his labor. He forbids the anxious insuring of oneself against the future by attempts to amass wealth, because he knows that man will set his heart on his treasure. He bids his reader not to be anxious about wealth, but rather to seek and establish God's righteousness in his heart and life. He counsels man to share with others as they have need, and such mutual help will afford one's life with stability against sickness and distress. Any attempt to gather wealth for one's self is condemned. If one is rich, he should use his wealth to raise the whole level of life

---

[54]Izzac Walton, *The Compleat Angler* (Fuildford, Surrey, G.B., 1962), ch. xxi.

for all, not just to raise himself above others. Are these thoughts idealistic? They are the thoughts of the inspired writer!

(7) Man In His Legal Relationships—The court of law had a special place in Hebraic tradition and thought. The court trial normally took place at the city's gate. No social situation reminded the Jew more strongly of his accountability as an Israelite than the court of law for it was at the "gate" that the Jew had to answer for his conduct as a responsible member of the community.

(i) The difficulty of judgment—It is often very difficult to decide who is guilty and who is innocent: "He who states his case first seems right, until the other comes and examines him" (Proverbs 18:17). A cross-examination often puts the plaintiff's case in a different light. We note here also that truth is many-sided. Even if one person may be right, it is highly possible that his fellow man, who rebuttals against him, may not be entirely wrong. It is imperative, therefore, that caution be utilized in all court room decisions. Sometimes our narrowness prevents us from seeing the various facets of truth. In all controversies we must learn to openly listen to both sides as we strive to bracket, or set aside, all preconceived ideas.

"The lot puts an end to disputes and decides between powerful contenders" (Proverbs 18:18). This proverb reveals an ancient method of arbitration used in deciding cases when no decision could be arrived at by the judges. This is the same end result of which the writer of the New Testament book of Hebrews addresses himself to when he writes, "Men indeed swear by a greater than themselves, and in all their disputes an oath is final for confirmation" (Hebrews 6:16). Whether or not a lot is used, the general lesson is, commit the decision to the wisdom of God. "The lot is cast into the lap, but the decision is wholly from the Lord" (Proverbs 16:33). Throughout the scriptures the casting of lots was used to determine the will of God (Leviticus 16:8; Numbers 26:55; Jonah 1:7; Acts 1:26).

"The partner of a thief hates his own life; he hears the curse, but discloses nothing" (Proverbs 29:24). In biblical times withholding evidence was also to be guilty of impeding justice. A partner in crime who refused to testify when called upon by the judge burdens his soul with the fact that he is guilty of a crime worthy of death. He becomes guilty of perjury and, in fact, sentences himself to the same fate as the criminal on trial. The law of Moses stated: "If any one sins in that he hears a public adjuration to testify and though he is a witness, whether he has seen or come to know the matter, yet does not speak, he shall bear his iniquity" (Leviticus 5:1).

"What your eyes have seen do not hastily bring into court; for what will you do in the end, when your neighbor puts you to shame? Argue your case with your neighbor himself, and do not disclose another's secret; lest he who hears you bring shame upon you, and your ill repute have no end" (Proverbs 25:7c-10). The advice is not to come to hasty conclusions concerning another's acts and bring such hasty conclusions to open court. Rather, discuss the matters in private and try to settle them in private if possible, lest one be brought to shame for having false testimony. Do not venture into any kind of strife for the result of such can only be bad. Some one has placed three tests in this matter: are the conclusions true—kind—necessary?

(ii) The object of punishment is to change the heart—To cause an individual to repent of past mis-deeds and change his ways is the end goal of all punishment: "Blows that wound cleanse away evil; strokes make clean the innermost parts" (Proverbs 20:30). Chastisement is good for the evil man for it deters him from further wrong-doing. Martin Luther taught, "Evil is cured, not by words, but by blows; suffering is as necessary as eating and drinking."

(8) Man In His Political Relationships—The Hebrew people maintained a theocratic philosophy of politics. Theocracy, or "God is king," may mean a society rigidly controlled by a caste of priests; or the equation may be "God is king, and the king is god," as was the situation in ancient Egypt. Then again, the rule of God may be reduced to a vague notion such as, "this nation, under God." The particular shape which the rule of God took in Israel, however, was the idea that God was in charge of the government and that the prophets and the kings were spokesmen of God. As with their spiritual and religious character, the political character of the Hebrew people was shaped by their views of God's involvement in their world. Whenever a prophet or king was supreme, his behavior tended to establish the moral code of the people in his domain for he spoke from God. In a theocracy, the behavior of God is the prototype of right behavior for the prophet or king. In reality, however, righteousness was often as capricious as the behavior of the prophet or king because these earthly rulers could never live up to the high righteousness manifested by the Lord God himself. The idea of the infallibility of the theocratic king is nowhere to be found in the scriptures. Still the ideal situation and

goal of the ruler was to live in harmony with God's righteousness as much as possible. Peace, justice and security were dependent on the willingness of the king to submit himself to the covenant of God. When this was lacking, the welfare of the people and the moral character of the nation was lost.

(i) The character of the king—Since the king was the spokesman of God, he had to be of a certain moral character if he were to lead his people in the ways of righteousness. The concern of the king had to be, first and foremost, the preservation of the moral standards of the nation in order that the nation might always maintain harmony with the covenant of their God and thus enjoy the security, blessings and protection which God offered. Realizing these grave responsibilities of the king, the writer of Proverbs gives some important advice:

(a) The king must deal righteously—"It is an abomination for kings to do evil, for the throne is established by righteousness" (Proverbs 16:12). Men in places of power often hold their positions with great uneasiness knowing that some other power-hungry individual might at any time dethrone them. The wise man urges here that the only real security for a king is for him to hold righteousness as the key theme in his reign. Only power that is guarded by righteousness and justice can hope for stability. The prophet Isaiah speaks of the results of such a reign of righteousness in Isaiah 32:1-8. In this passage, the prophet notes that the whole society will experience the purifying influence of the righteous king. "Righteousness exalts a nation" (Proverbs 14:34).

"Loyalty and faithfulness preserve the king, and his throne is upheld by righteousness" (Proverbs 20:28). From this proverb we note that loyalty and faithfulness are two spirits that guard the righteous king. Isaiah assures his readers that the king's throne is supported "with justice and with righteousness" (Isaiah 9:7). These are the safeguards of the power that deals with his subjects in wisdom. As Kilpatrick says, when the "rulers cease to be tyrants and become friends and protectors of men; there is an immediate quickening of the moral perception of the people, rash judgments are restrained and moral timidity give place to confidence. . . . It is no longer a question of wealth or poverty, of power or servitude, but of right or wrong, of noble personality or of evil."[55] Truly,

---

[55]G. G. D. Kilpatrick, *The Interpreter's Bible,* Volume 5, Isaiah (Nashville, 1956), p. 342.

"By justice a king gives stability to the land" (Proverbs 29:4), and also to his own reign.

(b) The king must be empathetic—The wise man emphasizes the need for the king to have a feeling for the problems of his subjects: "When the righteous are in authority, the people rejoice; and when the wicked rule, the poor groan. . . . If a king judges the poor with equity his throne will be established forever" (Proverbs 29:2, 14). The government must be the instrument that maintains a concern for the rights and needs of all classes. A throne built upon the gratitude and loyalty of the people will defy the storms of revolution. Once again we see the importance of righteousness and politics. The righteousness of the king can do so much to promote stability and peace within the nation.

(c) The king must punish the wicked—"A wise king winnows the wicked, and drives the wheel over them" (Proverbs 20:26). This wheel is probably a reference to the heavy iron-shod sledges with jagged teeth which were used to cut straw to pieces and thresh out the grain (cf Isaiah 28:27-28; Amos 1:3). It could also refer to the custom of the victorious king who drove his chariot over his prostrate enemies. In either case, it symbolizes the necessity of the king in conquering evil-doers. Such an illustration points to the severe punishment the king was to use in order to be a terror to those who violate the rights of their neighbor. In the New Testament, the apostle Paul says, "For rulers are not a terror to good conduct, but to bad" (Romans 13:3).

(ii) The duties of the people to their king—Christians are well aware of their responsibilities toward the state. These responsibilities are clearly outlined by the apostle Paul in Romans 13:1-7 (cf Ecclesiastes 8:2-5; 1 Timothy 2:1-2; Titus 3:1; 1 Peter 2:17). This same apostle assures Christians that "there is no authority except from God, and those that exist have been instituted by God" (Romans 13:1). This attitude of responsibility towards government was not just a Christian idea, however, for it was a prevalent philosophy in the Old Testament period of history also. The Hebrew king had the responsibility of caring for the people of God with power delegated to him from the Lord: "And he shall stand and feed his flock in the strength of the Lord, in the majesty of the name of the Lord his God. And they shall dwell secure, for now he shall be great to the ends of the earth" (Micah 5:4). But the people had a responsibility also; they would be required to give allegiance to the divinely instituted kingship for, "he shall be great to the ends of the earth." According to Proverbs, the duties of the people to the king are as follows:

(a) The people must support a righteous ruler—"In a multitude of people is the glory of a king, but without people a prince is ruined" (Proverbs 14:28). It is obvious that the strength and permanence of any ruler is dependent upon the loyalty of his subjects. It is not conquest, wealth, or power that makes a king great, but the loyalty of the people who support him and his policies. The king requires good, strong support from his subjects, and a wise king seeks to gain such support.

(b) Be patient and kind to the king—In reasoning with one of higher authority, there is a great need for patience and kindness: "With patience a ruler may be persuaded, and a soft tongue will break a bone" (Proverbs 25:15). By dispassionate calmness and a lack of wrath, one who stands before a king can persuade and win the favor of that ruler far quicker than the indecent and boisterous person. A person who carefully weighs his language and his words will have power when he speaks. We note the great contrast between Jesus and his accusers as both parties stood before Pilate. No doubt it was Jesus' bearing that so impressed Pilate and made him seek to win his release rather than crucify him.

(c) Hold the king in highest respect—"My son, fear the Lord and the king, and do not destroy either of them; for disaster from them will rise suddenly, and who knows what pain will come from them both" (Proverbs 24:21-22). Notice that obedience to God *and* the king are enjoined here. The apostle Peter uses this idea as a sign of godliness: "Honor all men. Love the brotherhood. Fear God. Honor the emperor" (1 Peter 2:17). The KJV of verse 21b means that one is to avoid any association with those who are of a revolutionary character in religion and politics.[56] This advise seems to counsel the acceptance of the *status quo* in government. Such would be good as long as the king is righteous, but there are times when the king may demand a citizen to believe or do what that citizen considers wrong. In such a situation it would be a sin to sit idly by and offer no resistance (*cf* Acts 4:18-20).

---

[56]"Them that are given to change" (verse 21b—KJV), is understood by Delitzsch (*ibid,* p. 138) to refer to dissidents, oppositionists, or revolutionaries, who fail to recognize the authority of the Lord or the king.

(d) The people must live righteously—It is important for the subjects of the king to live righteous lives for righteousness brings prosperity to a nation: "Righteousness exalts a nation, but sin is a reproach to any people" (Proverbs 14:34). Only when both the ruler and the ruled govern their actions by righteousness can there by any chance for real peace and order within the land. When justice and righteousness are the characteristic mark of the people, the nation will achieve the highest status of nationhood. The secret of a great nation is not wealth, power or tradition—it is righteousness in the lives of its leaders and citizens. Whereas sin is a nation's shame, righteousness is a nation's strength.

In speaking of national righteousness, Adeney says well, "It is forgotten that the ten commandments relate to communities as well as to individuals, because they are based on the eternal and all-embracing principles of righteousness. Men have yet to learn that which is wrong for the individual is wrong in the soceity. Nations make war on one another for reasons which would never justify individual men in fighting a duel. Yet if it is wrong for a man to steal a field, it must be wrong for a nation to steal a province. If an individual may not cut his neighbor's throat out of revenge without being punished as a criminal, there is nothing to justify a whole community in shooting down thousands of people for no better motive. If selfishness is sinful in one man, selfishness cannot be virtuous in thirty millions of people. The reign of righteousness must govern public and national movements if the will of God is to be respected."[57]

(9) Man's Duty To Animals—The relationship of man to the rest of the creation is set forth in Genesis 1:26: "Let them have dominion over the fish of the sea, and over the birds of the air, and over the cattle, and over all the earth, and over every creeping thing that creeps upon the earth." As with all responsibilities, there will also be a day of accountability. Man must enter into his lordship over the created world with a dead seriousness. What man must realize is that the "things" of the world over which he has dominion are the "things" of value in the sight of God for he made them. Thus, they deserve to be treated with the highest regard. This does not mean that man should romanticize or humanize plants

---

[57] W. F. Adeney, Homiletics in *The Pulpit Commentary,* Vol. 9, "Proverbs" (Grand Rapids, 1962), p. 281.

and animals, but that he must understand that God has made these things and they deserve such respect because he made them for what they are. It is not wrong to kill animals or cut down trees. But, if man kills, for example, an animal, he must kill it for a God-directed use (*ie,* for food, or clothing, *etc*). If a man cuts down a tree, he is not cutting down a person, but a tree, and he is using it in its God-designed use (heat or building, *etc*). God desires that we deal with plants as plants, animals as animals, machines as machines, and men as men. We must treat each thing in God's creation with integrity in its own order. Why? ". . . for the highest reason: because I love God—I love the One who has made it! Loving the Lover who has made it, I have respect for the thing He has made."[58] What does the book of Proverbs tell us about our duty toward animals?

(i) Man must regard animals—"A righteous man has regard for the life of his beast, but the mercy of the wicked is cruel" (Proverbs 12:10). The law of Moses specifically enjoined that kindness and mercy be shown to the animal world (*cf* Deuteronomy 25:4; Leviticus 22:28). The unrighteous man treats all things as objects to be used for his benefit, rather than as subjects to be regarded. In contrast, God has concern for all his works, both men and beasts (*cf* Psalms 36:6; 145:9; Jonah 4:11). The Lord even decreed that the rest of the sabbath was to be extended to domestic animals (Exodus 20:10); that a man should aid the overburdened beast (Exodus 34:4-5); that the unequaled strength of the ox and the ass should not be yoked together (Deuteronomy 22:10); that the ox should not be muzzled when treading out the corn (Deuteronomy 22:6); that a bird should not be taken from its young brood (Deuteronomy 22:6); nor a kid boiled in its mother's milk (Exodus 23:19). God helps those who cannot help themselves. When his creation is exploited, an affront has been committed against him, since he has created all things as ends and not as objects to be used.

In the prophetic books of the Old Testament, the prophet Jonah reflects God's concern for his created beings when he writes the thoughts of God: "And should not I pity Nineveh, that great city, in which there are more than a hundred and twenty thousand

---

[58]Francis A. Schaeffer, *Pollution and the Death of Man, The Christian View of Ecology* (Wheaton, Ill., 1970), *p* 57.

108

persons who do not know their right hand from their left, and also much cattle?'' (Jonah 4:11). Jesus, likewise, spoke of God's concern for his creation when he spoke of the flowers of the field and the lower creatures of the world (Matthew 6:25-30; 10:29). God is concerned for the birds of the air and the lilies of the field. Should not man manifest this same care and concern? To fail to show such concern is to reveal a base nature.

"Know well the condition of your flocks, and give attention to your herds" (Proverbs 27:23). Here is a proverb that exhorts a man to care diligently for his flock. Of course, the main emphasis in this passage is that if a man cares for his flock he will be richly blessed in an economic manner. Without the watchful care on the shepherd's part, the flock will be sickly and small. But, at the same time, we see here the proper interplay of man's labor and reward and God's provision for the good of both man and animal.

(10) Man's Duty To Himself—Man is the crown and center of creation. He was made in the image and likeness of God (Genesis 1:26) for fellowship with God, and as such man has great worth in God's sight. The most notable expression of the worth of man in God's sight is found in Psalms 8, which reveals that God grants to man royal honors and a status a little less than divine.[59] Man has been appointed to a place in the world of royal status; he is crowned with glory and honor. His affinity is with the Creator, not with the created; he is a little less than God.

Because man is placed in such a supreme position in relation to the rest of the creation, he is also placed in a responsible position. He has a place in history and is responsible to God for his conduct. As with all responsibility, he it is to whom much is given and of whom assuredly much will be required. Man is summoned by God, both to worship him as Lord and to practice righteousness toward his fellowman. Aside from his duties and responsibilities to God, however, are his duties and responsibilities to himself. Amid all the other responsibilities that man has outside himself, there are also responsibilities that man has to himself—responsibilities that are nonetheless important. What does the book of Proverbs tell us about the duties of man to himself?

(i) Self-control—Self-control is what the modern man needs the most, yet wants the least. The tragedy of the modern world is that

---
[59]The KJV has "angels"; the RSV has "God in Psalms 8:5. The Hebrew word is *elohim*, "God," the plural form of that word.

man is the master of so many things, yet has not yet learned to master himself. In the broadest sense, self-control describes the mastery of the appetites. It is the outgrowth of wisdom and knowledge. Guided by godly wisdom and knowledge, the wise man disciplines his appetites and makes them his servant rather than his master. In the midst of a world bent on striving for the road of self-indulgence and the way of least resistance, is the need for sacrifice, discipline and restraint. In the shallowness of a society based on pampering mankind comes a dire need for disciplined living. Realizing that it is only by consistent disciplined living that strength of character can be developed, the book of Proverbs encourages man to exercise self-control in the following areas of life:

(a) Sleep[60]—"Love not sleep, lest you come to poverty; open your eyes, and you will have plenty of bread" (Proverbs 20:13). The secret of success is to be vigilant and active in all things for "drowsiness will clothe a man with rags" (Proverbs 23:21). God provides man with abilities and opportunities but the individual must make proper use of them. Too many individuals permit their love for sleep to allow their opportunities to slip away little by little. While sleep has the advantage of renewing and refreshing the body, too much sleep will destroy. Like a robber, sleep brings poverty.

Another passage relating to the ill effects of a lack of self-control in respect to sleep is found in Proverbs 6:9-11:

> How long will you lie there, O sluggard?
>   When will you arise from your sleep?
> A little sleep, a little slumber,
>   a little folding of the hands to rest,
> and poverty will come upon you like a vagabond,
>   and want like an armed man.

This points out the biblical truth, "He who is slack in his work is a brother to him who destroys" (Proverbs 18:9). While the indolent person may not physically destroy, he does refuse to create, so in reality he is like the person who destroys. Curtailing production has the same effect as destroying something which has been produced.

---

[60]See subject study on labor, laziness and poverty, *pp* 94-97.

(b) Eating—"If you have found honey, eat only enough for you, lest you be sated with it and vomit it" (Proverbs 25:16). In a world with "nearly half a billion people . . . suffering from some form of hunger; 10,000 dying of starvation each week in Africa, Asia, and Latin America. . .,"[61] gluttony is a social problem. Mahatma Gandhi said well, "The earth provides enough for every man's need, but not for every man's greed." Moderation on the part of all and the sharing of what one has will do much to alleviate the hunger problem in our world.

But not only is gluttony a problem in the social environment, it is also a spiritual problem for it robs God of our usefulness and energy needed to work in his kingdom. Taylor wrote that, "eating is not a sin but gluttony is. The person who is habitually, self-indulgent in eating . . . without regard to health or need, almost as if he lived to eat rather than ate to live, is very apt to be weak and exposed in other phases of his life. Flabbiness in one area of character tends to loosen the whole."[62] The disciplined man will do as Daniel and his friend in relation to King Nebuchadnezzar's food, that is, control their intake to what is proper and good (Daniel 1:21). New Testament references to such discipline are numerous (Romans 12:1-2; 1 Corinthians 3:16-17; 6:19-20; 9:26-27; 2 Timothy 2:4; Hebrews 12:1; etc).

Self-control in relation to eating is emphasized again in Proverbs 23:1-2: "When you sit down to eat with a ruler, observe carefully what is before you; and put a knife to your throat if you are a man given to appetite." The expression "a knife to your throat," refers to self-control, the ability to restrain oneself in the midst of a great variety of food and drink (cf Ecclesiasticus 31:12-18). Appetite filled can be a constant source of pleasure, but like all pleasures, there is always the temptation to excessiveness.

(c) Worldly pleasure—"He who loves pleasure will be a poor man; he who loves wine and oil will not be rich" (Proverbs 21:17). Pleasure-seeking destroys a man financially, intellectually, and spiritually. James, the writer of the New Testament epistle, informs us that "friendship with the world is enmity with God" (James 4:4). Worldly pleasure, of course, refers to illegitimate pleasure for nowhere in the scriptures, Old or New Testament, is it taught

---

[61]Hal Lindsay, *The Terminal Generation* (Old Tappan, N.J., 1974), p. 62.
[62]Richard Shelley Taylor, *The Disciplined Life* (Minneapolis, 1962), p. 92.

that all pleasure is wrong or improper. Pleasure, when chosen wisely and used in moderation, may do much to mitigate the rigors of life, but when sought as the end goal, it is destructive. So here, as in other areas, moderation is essential.

It is well to contrast Proverbs 21, verses 15 and 17: "When justice is done, it is a joy to the righteous. . . . He who loves pleasure will be a poor man." The just and righteous man seeks to deal fairly, and finds joy for himself. In contrast, the pleasure-seeker devotes himself to finding joy for himself, and finds poverty instead—the greatest of poverty—that poverty of spirit which comes from pleasure-seeking. He may gain the pleasures of the world, yet lose out on the chief pleasure, that being an eternal fellowship with his Creator.

(d) Wine—The wise men of Israel were keenly aware of the dangers of strong drink and in Proverbs 23:29-35 they give a vivid and graphic description of the plight of the drunkard. There are several reasons given for drinking. Some drink for the momentary pleasure, but the wise man warns, "At last it bites like a serpent, and stings like an adder" (Proverbs 23:32). Here, the social and moral consequences of excessive drinking are compared to the sting of a deadly serpent. Drinking is also viewed as a way of escape from a bad situation, a way "to get away from it all." This may bring temporary relief, but bitter is the return to the world of reality.

The characteristics of the excessive drinker are vividly set forth by the writer of Proverbs in chapter 23:29-35. The problem drinker has sorrow, redness of eyes, hallucinations and bodily ills and torments. The more comical characteristics, comical if they were not so tragic, are that the drunkard swaggers like a sailor tossed at sea; he is physically beaten, yet does not feel the pain so that he might avoid harm; and in the midst of all this, the first thing he desires when he awakens after all these encounters is a drink of wine: "When shall I awake? I will seek another drink" (Proverbs 23:35).

Proverbs warns rulers about the use of alcohol for alcohol breeds irresponsibility: "It is not for kings, O Lemuel, it is not for kings to drink wine, or for rulers to desire strong drink; lest they drink and forget what has been decreed, and pervert the rights of all the afflicted" (Proverbs 31:4-5). To properly govern a people requires intelligence, ability and discipline, marks not characteristic of the one addicted to wine. The problems caused by rulers given to much wine are readily seen in several biblical examples such as, Elah of 1 Kings 16:8-9; Benhadad of 1 Kings 20:16; and Belshazzar of Daniel 5:2-4 (*cf* Genesis 9:20-23; 19:32-38; Isaiah 5:1-12, 22; 28:1, 7-8; Jeremiah 23:9; Hosea 7:5; Amos 6:6).

The problems of alcoholism take on new dimensions in our modern age, especially when we think of the drinking driver, air line pilot, or surgeon. The advice of the wise man to the ruler about the necessity of a clear mind in his judgements certainly apply to those who command cars and airplanes, and to those who perform surgery. It is clearly evident that the evil consequences resulting from drunkenness does not fall on the drunken man alone, but also on the lives of all people he may come into contact with. The alcoholic is a threat to the society; he costs taxpayers for his exploits are involved in accidents, crimes, marriage breakups, etc. Alcohol remains the number one drug problem in America today with over nine million people in this country who are alcoholics or dependent on alcohol.[63] Truly alcohol "bites like a serpent, and stings like an adder" (Proverbs 23:32).

How do we combat the evil effects of alcohol? Prohibition is not the answer if there is no general disposition to support such a law. Maybe the solution lies in prohibiting the sale of alcoholic beverages for profit. The brewer must sell his products and so spends incredible amounts of money advertising and making his products attractive. It may be a man's business if he wants to take a drink, but it should not be someone's business to encourage others to drink in order to realize personal profit.

The best safeguard against alcohol is not to drink at all, for "wine is a mocker, strong drink a brawler; and whoever is led astray by it is not wise" (Proverbs 20:1). "Do not look at wine when it is red" (Proverbs 23:31). Winston Churchill says that he once asked Bernard Shaw, "Do you really never drink any wine at all?" Shaw replied, "I am hard enough to keep in order as it is."[64] So many have been turned into fools by not being able to handle strong drink. Thus, the wise man avoids the use of alcohol altogether.

From the above emphasis on the evils of wine, we must not take the attitude that wine is altogether to be condemned. It was

[63]Albert Q. Maisel, "Alcohol and Your Brain," *The Reader's Digest,* June, 1970.
[64]Winston Churchill, *Great Contemporaries* (New York, 1937), p. 35.

considered both good and evil in the Old and New Testaments. Wine was a common drink within the nation of God's people. It was used in sacrifices and offerings (Numbers 28:14); it was taken with meals, served on feast days and at weddings (John 2:1-10). Wine was also used as a medicine for various internal disorders (Luke 5:37-39; 10:34; 1 Timothy 5:23). Thus, wine can be listed among the good gifts to man from God. The Psalmist refers to God giving "wine to gladden the heart of man" (Psalms 104:15; cf Judges 9:13).

Christians are urged to be moderate in their use of wine, to avoid the sins of excess and self-indulgence (1 Timothy 3:2-3, 8, 11; Titus 2:1-3). That our Lord used wine is without question (Luke 7:33-34), yet it would be absurd to think that he was ever guilty of excess or self-indulgence. So, while it is not sin to drink alcoholic beverages, the wise man will give serious attention to Paul's words: "Do not get drunk with wine, for that is debauchery; but be filled with the Spirit" (Ephesians 5:18).

(e) Anger—There is a great deal in Proverbs concerning the problem of anger. "A man of quick temper acts foolishly, but a man of discretion is patient" (Proverbs 14:17). A common mark of man is the powerful emotion of anger which is so easily aroused at times due to some personal offense. It is the wise man who is able to exercise self-control in temperance. While such is not an easy characteristic to acquire, it is certainly vital in living a proper life in relation to our neighbors and God.

"He who is slow to anger is better than the mighty, and he who rules his spirit than he who takes a city" (Proverbs 16:32). It is a credit to one's ability of self-control that he is slow to anger. In fact, it is better to hold in check one's anger than it is to gain control over the riches and nations of this world. Mighty military men have conquered cities and nations, enslaving and controlling millions, yet they have been unable to control their own passions. A great leader without a well-balanced temper is always in danger of rendering poor judgment due to mental faculties being disturbed by anger or due to the loss of true proportion. It is said that Alexander, who conquered the world, was a slave to anger and in the midst of an outrage killed a close and intimate friend, Clytus.[65] In contrast to this, the disciplined man who controls his anger has the highest kind of power and can be trusted to rule over others because he has

---

[65]Adam Clarke, op. cit., p. 749.

learned how to rule himself. As the Chinese say, "Who can govern himself is fit to govern the world."

Too many individuals today are "too soon angry," and as a result stir up so much unnecessary contention and strife. "A hot tempered man stirs up strife" (Proverbs 15:18). It is doubtful that anything constructive is ever said when people are angry. Anger has a way of removing reason from the heart. It often produces a desire to hurt—a desire to get even. Someone has well said, "It wouldn't hurt so much to become angry, except that, for some reason, anger makes your mouth work faster than your mind."

In stressing the importance of thinking before speaking, the wise man exhorts: "He who restrains his words has knowledge, and he who has a cool spirit is a man of understanding. Even a fool who keeps silent is considered wise; when he closes his lips, he is deemed intelligent" (Proverbs 17:27-28). A man who is angry is seldom able to restrain his speech and, therefore, speaking without thinking, will get into trouble. Once words have been spoken, they cannot be recalled. It has been reported that Abraham Lincoln remarked: "Better to remain silent and be thought a fool than to speak out and remove all doubt."

"A man without self-control is like a city broken into and left without walls" (Proverbs 25:28). The man who puts no restraint on his anger is always in danger of being carried away by it. A lack of self-control nearly always involves sin and destruction. An angered individual is constantly undefended and open to invasion by his enemy, anger. We need to concentrate on using words that bring help and wholeness to others. We need to use words that reflect what we are in the inner depths of our being. Yet such is very difficult to do if we allow ourselves to speak forth in anger. Our words come out of the heart and reflect the real man, thus we must cultivate a calmness that brings forth life and health. Jesus Christ taught that "what comes out of the mouth proceeds from the heart, and this defiles a man. For out of the heart come evil thoughts, murder, adultery, fornications, theft, false witness, slander. These are what defile a man . . ." (Matthew 15:18-20).

"A fool gives full vent to his anger, but a wise man quietly holds it back" (Proverbs 29:11). A foolish man reveals everything he thinks or feels in his anger. The Preacher wisely writes that there is "a time to keep silence, and a time to speak" (Ecclestiastes 3:7b). Few are not without the need to be urged to keep on guard in relation to anger. Self-control is not an easy characteristic to acquire, but it is certainly vital in living the proper life in the sight of God and man. Self-control in speech is a wonderful and much to be desired attribute. As James says, "For we all make many mistakes, and if anyone makes no mistakes in what he says he is a perfect man, able to bridle the whole body also" (James 3:2).

We must not deceive ourselves into thinking that all anger is bad, however. Jesus became angry on several occasions, but never for the purpose of having his own way. In Mark 3:1-6, Jesus looked upon the crowd with anger because they were critically watching to see if he would heal the man with a withered hand on the sabbath. His anger was just for it was mingled with grief due to the hardness and blindness of the people. This righteous anger is revealed again in Matthew 21:12-13 when Jesus drove the money-changers and tradesmen from the temple. We are also reminded of the apostle Paul's words: "Be angry but do not sin; do not let the sun go down on your anger, and give no opportunity to the devil" (Ephesians 4:26-27).

We recognize, then, that anger is not in itself evil. Jesus' anger was never directed against innocent people. He did not say harsh things to those that were not deserving. We never see anything selfish in his anger; it was always righteous. Jesus' anger was never intemperate, violent or destructive. It was always motivated by anguish in his heart over injustice being done to God's will or God's children. Thus, the wise man will keep his anger and tongue under control, even when wronged. He will strive to be as God, "merciful and gracious, slow to anger, and abounding in steadfast love and faithfulness" (Exodus 34:6). For other references on anger see: Proverbs 14:29; 15:1; 19:11, 19; 26:11; 29:20.

(ii) Attitude toward temptation—The impulse for an individual to do evil is often attributed by the scriptures to Satan. In the New Testament, the apostle Peter warns, "Be sober, be watchful. Your adversary the devil prowls around like a roaring lion, seeking someone to devour" (1 Peter 5:8). Paul also warns against the powers of the devil in tempting man when he writes to the Thessalonians, "I sent that I might know your faith, for fear that somehow the tempter had tempted you and that our labor would be in vain" (1 Thessalonians 3:5). And in Ephesians 6:10, this same apostle urges, "Put on the whole armor of God, that you may be able to stand against the wiles of the devil."

From these teachings we note that Satan's purpose is to lead men and women of God to do evil. The thing that we often fail to realize, however, is that the ultimate blame for sin must rest upon man. James writes, 'Let no one say when he is tempted, 'I am tempted by God'; for God cannot be tempted with evil and he himself tempts no one, but each person is tempted when he is lured and enticed by his own desire" (James 1:13-14). In this same vein, Thomas Aquinas argued that since man has the power to say "Yes" or "No" to temptation, that he must share the responsibility for any sin. Realizing this, what does the book of Proverbs teach about one's attitude toward temptation?

(a) Man must flee temptation—The wise man strongly urges against associations with the wicked:

"Do not enter the path of the wicked
and do not walk in the way of evil men.
Avoid it; do not go on it;
turn away from it and pass on.
For they cannot sleep unless they have done wrong;
they are robbed of sleep unless they have made someone stumble.
For they eat the bread of wickedness
and drink the wine of violence" (Proverbs 4:14-17).

One of the greatest illustrations of continuing resistance against the temptation to do wrong is the story of Joseph and Potiphar's wife (Genesis 39:6-23). It was probably not too difficult for Joseph to say no to the advances of Potiphar's wife the first time or two, but later, as she continually pursued him, it must have been extremely difficult. Joseph knew that he must remain faithful to God, however, so we read that he "fled and got out of the house" (Genesis 39:12b).

In relation to associations with the wicked, the wise man exhorts, "Be not envious of evil men, nor desire to be with them; for their minds devise violence, and their lips talk of mischief" (Proverbs 24:1-2; cf Proverbs 2:31; 23:17). This is the same advice given by the apostle Paul: "Do not be deceived: 'Bad company ruins good morals' " (1 Corinthians 15:33). We become like those we associate with, therefore, to associate with the sinful makes us like them and a partner in their workings. In a world where it appears many times that the wicked prosper and the righteous suffer, it is so easy to envy the wicked. Such envy, however, is short-lived for "the wages of sin is death" (Romans 6:23). The sage reminds us: "Fret not yourself because of evildoers, and be not envious of the wicked; for the evil man has no future; the lamp of the wicked will be put out" (Proverbs 24:19-20).

One of the problems that Job faced had to do with the prosperity of the wicked. He could not understand why the wicked seemed to live, grow old, and even become greater in power (Job 21:7-18), while the innocent perish. He questioned the justice of God in such situations: "How often is it that the lamp of the wicked is put out?" (Job 21:7), Job asked. "Not very often," concluded Job. The patriarch was later led by God to recognize that the affairs of the world are in the hands of a just and loving Creator who does not necessarily move according to the dictates of man. Part of man's arrogance is that he thinks he can control and know the affairs of the world, as well as his own destiny. Faith however, asks us to believe and trust that everything God allows is right and for the highest good of his people (cf Romans 8:28). The wicked may enjoy prosperity for a season, but there is no hope for them in the future.

(b) Man is to resist temptation—"The beginning of strife is like letting out water; so quit before the quarrel breaks out" (Proverbs 17:14). It is so very difficult to turn the other cheek, to walk away from a fight; and so it is just as difficult to avoid or resist temptation. To be subject to God, however, entails resistance to evil. If one allows evil to become a part of his life, that evil has a tendency to grow and take possession of other areas of life. Evil is defeated, however, by a steadfast resistance and it will be conquered when resisted. God promises that he will not allow the Christian to be tempted above that which the Christian is able to bear (1 Corinthians 10:13), and that he is able to keep the Christian from falling (Jude 24-25).

(11) Man's duty to others—Long ago, in the Garden of Eden, Cain uttered those famous words to God in relation to his brother, Abel, "Am I my brother's keeper?" (Genesis 4:9b). His brother's keeper is exactly what Cain should have been, and it is exactly what we must be. Sooner or later, men must realize that any cruelty, unkindness, or unconcern manifested toward a fellow human being brings them face to face with God's judgment. Jesus taught this great truth when he gave the two great commandments: "You shall love the Lord your God with all your heart, and with all your soul, and with all your mind. This is the great and first commandment. And a second is like it, You shall love your

neighbor as yourself" (Matthew 22:37-39). Jesus clearly reveals that we have a duty toward others, a duty which involves a willingness to take the time and effort to establish personal relationships with others. Tragically, most are not willing to do this, and so, go through life with no real sense of responsibility to others.

What prevents us from developing personal relationships with others, which, in turn, prevents us from fulfilling our role as our brother's keeper? In many cases, it is caused by being too enclosed within the narrow circle of our own interests, ambitions and activities. In isolation from other people, how is one ever to become aware of their needs? If we fail to associate with the poor, sick, outcasts, publicans and unrighteous ones of the world, or even our neighbors who share a similar situation in life with us how will we know their needs? Even if by some chance their needs are thrust upon us, we do not feel them as we feel our own because we do not have a relationship with them. And so, the word of God has a great deal to say about, not the great sinners of the world, but about those who ignore their fellowmen and take not even a little interest in serving their needs.

In order to combat this tendency to isolate ourselves from our neighbor and thus fail to "love our neighbor as ourself," we must learn of our duties and responsibilities toward our neighbor and, then, establish relationships with him. We must avoid the tendency to be separated from our neighbor by artificial barriers of wealth, class or self-centeredness. Jesus taught this explicitly (Luke 14:12-14). The test of love for neighbor, the second greatest commandment in the world, and the way to fulfillment of God's will for our lives, is found in a willingness, at some cost of time, money and effort, to give practical assistance to our fellowman. Proverbs has several things to say concerning our duty and responsibility to others. These areas of responsibility are as follows:

(i) Evils to avoid—When dealing with others, there are several evils to avoid in order to establish personal relationships with them. If we are to grow in a knowledge of our neighbor, knowing his interests, hopes, fears, joys and sorrows, we must avoid certain things which might hinder the development of such necessary relationships. These evils to avoid are:

(a) Avoid belittling—To depreciate one's neighbor is one of the greatest hindrances to establishing relationships. "He who belittles his neighbor lacks sense, but a man of understanding remains silent" (Proverbs 11:12). Just as we do not believe all that we hear, we should not speak all that we know. A good piece of advice is, "Always tell the truth, but don't always be telling it" (*cf* Ecclesiasticus 19:7-10). Friendship must be nurtured, cared for and protected. Part of this development process requires that we not belittle, especially if such is harmful. Granted, there are times when we must tell the truth in love; times when we must point out certain defects within the life of others; but belittling does not promote love. Adam Clarke says, "A man of understanding—a prudent sensible man, hides those defects wherever he can, and puts the most charitable construction on those which he cannot conceal."[66] We need to weigh well the impact of our words before we speak. We must use gracious and kind words when speaking about others.

(b) Avoid greed—"A greedy man stirs up strife, but he who trusts in the Lord will be enriched" (Proverbs 28:25). The desire to be preeminent and first in all things has led many a man into ruin. In the New Testament, James writes on the evils of greed: "What causes wars, and what causes fightings among you? Is it not your passions that are at war in your members? You desire and do not have; so you kill. And you covet and cannot obtain; so you fight and wage war. You do not have because you do not ask. You ask and do not receive, because you ask wrongly, to spend it on your passions" (James 4:1-3). There are so many relationships broken due to the struggle for first place on the part of many. Greed for first place and first things in the social, political, and even religious circles of life, produce the oppression, hatred and lack of brotherly concern so prevalent in our world. The non-greedy, God-fearing individual, on the other hand, does much to promote peace and fulfill his responsibilities toward God and his brother.

(c) Avoid returning evil for evil—"Be not a witness against your neighbor without cause, and do not deceive with your lips. Do not say, 'I will do to him as he has done to me; I will pay the man back for what he has done' " (Proverbs 24:28-29; *cf* Proverbs 17:5; 20:22; 23:17; 25:21-22). This is one of the high points in the moral and ethical teachings of the Old Testament. The false accuser has always been an abomination to God (*cf* Deuteronomy 19:18-21) due to the evil effects of such testimony. We note also the emphasis against retaliation, which seems to go contrary to the Deuteronomic law. The law, however, was meant to limit vengeance. The judge

---

[66]Adam Clarke, op. cit., p. 733.

fixed the penalty for the situation and it is doubtful that the full legal penalty was exacted in all situations. The writer of Proverbs seems to transcend this "eye for eye, tooth for tooth," concept and certainly it was superceded by Jesus Christ who asserted that love, not just retaliation, fulfills the deeper intent of God's will (Matthew 5:38-41).

(d) Flattery—"A man who flatters his neighbor spreads a net for his feet" (Proverbs 29:5). Flattery is a deadly vice that can affect the whole of life. It can give an individual a false impression of himself. Few people can retain a wholesome and balanced view of themselves when they give in to the praise of a flatter. It is so easy to lose one's perspective in the midst of praise. While it is true that one should emphasize the good and positive in the lives of others, it is wrong and misleading to whitewash the unworthy things. As the Psalmist says, "May the Lord cut off all flattering lips" (Psalms 12:3).

"He who rebukes a man will afterward find more favor than he who flatters with his tongue" (Proverbs 28:23). Friendship must be built on gentleness and concern, but one who points out weaknesses and strengths in a friend is of far greater value than one who flatters to maintain a friendship. It may hurt one's pride to be corrected, but the end result will be the betterment of one's life and character. James writes: "My brethren, if any one among you wanders from the truth and some one brings him back, let him know that whoever brings back a sinner from the error of his way will save his soul from death and will cover a multitude of sins" (James 5:19-20). The end goal of all constructive criticism is to make the person a better individual, and if one desires to change any individual, without giving offense or arousing resentment, one must begin with honest praise and appreciation. After this, carefully and tactfully point out weaknesses. (For other benefits of praise and dangers of flattery see: Proverbs 15:5, 12; 25:12; 26:27; 27:5-6; 28:10; 29:5.)

(e) Avoid gossip—Unkind gossip is a deadly use of the tongue and is not just limited to the passing on of falsehood about others either. The talebearer may be telling the truth about another person, yet be just as deadly. No individual is perfect and some are guilty of sins that have a greater social disapproval than others. In such situations, one is well-informed when he maintains silence. The writer of Proverbs has this to say about gossip: Proverbs 26:20-26. Henry van Dyke set forth rules in relation to gossip: "Never believe anything bad about any one unless you positively know it is true; never tell even that unless you feel that it is absolutely necessary; and remember that God is listening while you tell it."

The greatest chapter in the Bible on love is the thirteenth chapter of 1 Corinthians. This chapter is one of the best known and best loved passages in the word of God. If man would abide by its great principles, he could solve most major problems in life and promote harmony in the world. Especially we note verse 6 of this chapter: "Love does not rejoice at wrong, but rejoices in the right. The apostle Paul's point here can be used to cover a variety of subjects, but surely it also covers the sin of gossip. Some of the greatest harm and damage is caused by the desire to talk. Much of this talk is done with little or no regard or thought for its end result.

One of the greatest ills of gossip is the assassination of reputations. Gossip is the most ruthless killer of reputations. It is an active, vicious, and destructive force that divides people. It promotes petty jealousy, envy, hatred and intolerance. A godly man must, therefore, use great caution in repeating tales concerning others. Before doing so, we must ask the following questions: Is it true? Is it necessary to repeat? Is it kind? A negative answer to any of these questions is just cause not to repeat the story.

One of the seven things which is an abomination to the Lord God is "a false witness who breathes out lies" (Proverbs 6:19). The inspired penman of the word of God says, "Love rejoices in the right" (1 Corinthians 13:6). The Psalmist says, "O Lord, who shall sojourn in thy tent? Who shall dwell on the holy hill? He who walks blamelessly, and does what is right, and speaks truth from his heart; who does not slander with his tongue, and does no evil to his friend, nor takes up a reproach against his neighbor . . ." (Psalms 15:1-3). "Finally, brethren, whatever is true, whatever is honorable, whatever is just, whatever is pure, whatever is lovely, whatever is gracious, if there is any excellence, if there is anything worthy of praise, think about these things" (Philippians 4:8).

Love cannot listen with pleasure nor repeat the story of another's moral failure. In *Midrash Rabbah,* Lev. 33:1, we read: "R. Simeon B. Gamaliel said to Tabbai his servant: 'Go and buy me good food in the market.' He went and brought him tongue. He said to him: 'Go and buy me bad food in the market.' Tabbai went and brought him tongue. Said he to him: "What is this? When I told you to get me good food you bought me tongue, and when I told you to get bad food you also bought me tongue!" Tabbai replied: 'Good comes from it and bad comes from it. When the tongue is good there is nothing better, and when it is bad there is nothing worse' '' (cf Proverbs 16:28; 11:13).

(ii) Virtues to cherish—In dealing with others, there is more to building successful relationships than just avoiding certain evils. We must also develop some positive principles which will help to build strong and enduring friendships. Our responsibility to love our neighbor as we love ourselves (Leviticus 19:17-18; Matthew 22:34-40) demands that we establish certain virtues in our life as we associate with our neighbor. Some of the virtues to cherish when dealing with our fellowman are:

(a) Be forgiving— "He who forgives an offense seeks love, but he who repeats a matter alienates a friend" (Proverbs 17:9). Nothing is more irritating than a person who continually "harpeth" (ASV) on a matter. Such an attitude soon destroys a friendship. Forgiveness is a very necessary and proper work of every man who desires to establish relationships that are worthwhile. The wise man urges his readers to make haste to forgive for it saves a friendship.

In the New Testament, Jesus taught, "If you forgive men their trespasses, your heavenly Father also will forgive you; but if you do not forgive men their trespasses, neither will your Father forgive your trespasses" (Matthew 6:14-15). Jesus also taught that there must be no limits to such forgiveness: "Peter came up and said to him, 'Lord how often shall my brother sin against me, and I forgive him? As many as seven times?' Jesus said to him, 'I do not say to you seven times, but seventy times seven' '' (Matthew 18:21-22). Individuals who have such great need for forgiveness (as we all do) certainly ought to be able to forgive others.

(b) Encourage rather than discourage—"He who sings songs to a heavy heart is like one who takes off a garment on a cold day, and like vinegar on a wound" (Proverbs 25:20). As has been pointed out before, it is important that we criticize to build up individuals, but constructive criticism must be well-timed. Schloerb writes, "The wise use of the tongue will include the difficult discipline of proper timing. One might think that truth is truth no matter when it is spoken, but if one is dealing with persons rather than with propositions, he will try to speak the truth when and where it is fitting and needed . . . . the right thing spoken at the wrong time can hardly be called 'a word fitly spoken' (Proverbs

25:11).''[67] There is a virtue in frankness, but it must be coupled with intelligence, tact and discretion.

The importance of exercising good judgment in the use of words and action is emphasized again: "A word spoken in due season, how good it is" (Proverbs 15:23). There is a proper time to speak and act. We should be aware of the wisdom of proper timing in order that we encourage and build up rather than tear down. Jesus utilized this principle when he told his disciples, "I have yet many things to say to you, but you cannot bear them now" (John 16:12). Paul urges Christians, "Rejoice with those who rejoice, weep with those who weep" (Romans 12:15). Words have great power in encouraging and uplifting: "There is one whose rash words are like sword thrusts, but the tongue of the wise brings healing" (Proverbs 12:18). Regardless of how disciplined a person is, the only true disciplined character is one whose tongue is restrained by prudence and love for others. "If any one thinks he is religious, and does not bridle his tongue but deceives his heart, this man's religion is vain" (James 1:26).

"A soft answer turns away wrath, but a harsh word stirs up anger" (Proverbs 15:1). Some would believe that a soft answer expresses a timidity that yields to unreasonable and impudent demands and opens the person up to more demands. Such is not true, however, for a righteous man who uses soft speech never compromises truth, nor does he yield up righteousness. A soft answer may be firm in substance and, as a result, will do much to turn away wrath. In contrast, harsh words only inflame the situation and produce hatred and more misery. One of the greatest unifying influences is a soft answer. When difficulties arise, as they will, it is the wise person that seeks to respond in kindness, not in kind. Such can be accomplished by the training of one's thoughts and attitudes toward others.

(c) Help those in need—"A man who is kind benefits himself, but a cruel man hurts himself" (Proverbs 11:17). Kindness is pictured as beneficial not only to the person who receives it but also to the one who practices it. Notice too, the emphasis on retributive justice. Kindness is commended because of the rewards it brings. Rewards for right living are often set forth to motivate men to follow after wisdom. This does not mean, however, that one is to

---

[67]Rolland W. Schloerb, *The Interpreter's Bible,* Volume IV (Nashville, 1955), p. 889.

124

devote himself to kindness for the sole motive of having a good life. Such a life will be rewarding, but it must be motivated by a desire to seek after wisdom, or the will of God. The quest for Godlike character is the highest incentive for helping others in need.

"One man gives freely, yet grows all the richer; another withholds what he should give, and only suffers want. A liberal man will be enriched, and one who waters will himself be watered. The people curse him who holds back grain, but a blessing is on the head of him who sells it" (Proverbs 11:24-26). Surely the greatest motive for helping others is in gratitude for what God has done for us. We can honor God only by meeting human needs as they arise. Sir Wilfred Grenfell wrote: "It is not the size nor the gold equivalent of what each of us contributes to the world that is a measure of the value of his gifts. The service we render to others is really the rent we pay for our room on this earth. It is obvious that man is himself a traveller; that the purpose of this world is not 'To have and to hold' but 'To give and to serve.' There can be no other meaning"[68]

(d) Return good for evil—"If your enemy is hungry, give him bread to eat; and if he is thirsty, give him water to drink; for you will heap coals of fire on his head, and the Lord will reward you" (Proverbs 25:21-22). This passage is quoted by the apostle Paul when he urges his fellow-Christians at Rome to forgo vengeance against their enemies (Romans 12:20). Some interpret this idea of heaping coals of fire upon another's head to mean the kindling of feelings of shame and self-reproach, which in turn can bring about a new relationship. It would certainly be wrong to have as a motive for treating an enemy with kindness, the desire to see him punished by having coals of fire heaped upon him. The motivating reason for treating an enemy with kindness is that of changing him from an enemy to a friend. Notice also that the emphasis here is not on passive non-resistance, but rather on active kindness. An old Chinese proverb reads: "I meet good with good, that good may be maintained; I meet evil with good, that good may be created." The high peak in the treatment of enemies is found in the lifestyle and teachings of Jesus: "I say to you, Love your enemies and pray for those who persecute you" (Matthew 5:44).

In relation to overcoming evil with good, the wise man also says,

---

[68]Sir Wilfred Grenfell, *A Labrador Lagbook* (Boston, 1938), p. 112.

"Do not rejoice when your enemy falls, and let not your heart be glad when he stumbles; lest the Lord see it, and be displeased, and turn away his anger from him" (Proverbs 24:17-18). Rejoicing over an enemy's tragedy cannot be the attitude of the wise man. Such is sure to be displeasing to the Lord God. The man of wisdom will continually strive to rise above that human tendency toward vindictiveness and retaliation.

NUMERICAL RIDDLES

Proverbs 30:11-31 is a collection of numerical proverbs like the one found in Proverbs 6:16-19. These proverbs list phenomena and observations based on the behavior of various creatures, behavior which teaches several truths that man needs to learn from. They describe some quality or character in terms of either warning or commendation, and in most of them the number four is conspicuous. In this section of study we will examine six groups of proverbs which use the number four.

(1) Four Classes of Evil Doers—This section of Proverbs 30 deals with four types of sinners, or generations (KJV as per the Hebrew text), to be avoided:

"There are those who curse their father
   and do not bless their mothers.
There are those who are pure in their own eyes
   but are not cleansed of the filth.
There are those—how lofty are their eyes,
   how high their eyelids lift!
There are those whose teeth are swords, whose teeth are knives
   to devour the poor from off the earth, the needy from
   among men." (Proverbs 30:11-14).

It is truly an evil generation that has no love and concern for its parents (verse 11). The fifth commandment given to Moses in the Mount was, "Honor your father and your mother, that your days may be long in the land which the Lord your God gives you" (Exodus 20:12). Under the law of Moses, a failure to obey and honor parents was a sin worthy of death (Exodus 21:17; cf Proverbs 20:20; 30:17). To the Jew, next to the sin of disobeying God was the sin of disobeying one's parents. This was because the father was considered the absolute authority in the home. To repudiate the father's authority represented the most grievous anarchy. Such led to ingratitude and the repudiation of God. The apostle Paul lists this sin among the sins to be associated with the last days: "But understand this, that in the last days there will come times of stress. For men will be lovers of self, lovers of money, proud, arrogant, abusive, disobedient to their parents . . ." (2 Timothy 3:1-2).

The second characteristic of the four classes of evil doers is that of spiritual pride (verse 12). How very easy it is for individuals to exalt themselves above others in the spiritual realm. The adoption of pious attitudes—that uplifted face and heart—that tends to look down on the spiritual resources of other people is truly an abomination in the sight of God. The wise man must avoid the desire to think too highly of himself, for whether one is superior or inferior to others is of no ultimate importance; what counts ultimately is how far short one falls from the divine perfection found in God. As Micah the prophet says so well, "He has showed you, O man, what is good; and what does the Lord require of you but to do justice, and to love kindness, and to walk humbly with your God?" (Micah 6:8).

The third characteristic of evil doers is that of pride and arrogance (verse 13; cf Proverbs 6:17; 8:13; 16:18; 21:4; 29:23). This sin is so deadly because it can operate in a person's heart while outwardly he appears to be a devout follower after God. It is the inordinate seeking after excellence; the love of self even to the contempt of God.[69] Although the word "pride" carries with it a negative connotation, it can be descriptive of self-respect, dignity, and satisfaction with one's situation in life. The wise man must distinguish between pride as the worship of the creature rather than the Creator, and pride as that self-respect without which no man can serve God. The life of the wise man is one in which pride as self-glorification is absent, but pride as genuine self-respect is a reality in his life.

The fourth class of evil doers are those who oppress the poor and helpless (verse 14). Such individuals exploit people, especially weaker people, and use them as objects to further selfish goals. From this we realize that social problems are also religious problems. God is deeply concerned with the poor and the helpless and takes

---

[69]A. Augustine, *City of God*, tr. John Healey (New York, 1957), XII, 13.

note when they are mistreated, neglected and oppressed. His concern is of such that he will not leave such individuals defenseless. This social injustice was the major problem that Amos addressed in his preaching to Israel. Religious zeal was very high in Israel as the people went on pilgrimages (Amos 4:4-5), had many festivals (Amos 5:21-24), spent large sums of money to build beautiful sanctuaries (Amos 7:13; 5:4-5), loved to assemble, pay tithes, offer sacrifices and sing praises to God (Amos 4:4-5; 5:21-23). Yet Amos declared that God does not accept the external worship of those who do not deal justly and righteously with their fellow man, particularly with the poor and needy. Quantity of sacrifice or money, loudness of singing, and length of prayers, are no substitutes for right attitudes and right behavior toward the poor and needy. Thus, the Proverbs writer, and the prophets, preach basically what James writes: "Religion that is pure and undefiled before God and the Father is this: to visit[70] orphans and widows in their affliction, and to keep oneself unstained from the world" (James 1:27). Man's inhumanity to man: a sin against God and man to be avoided by the wise man.

(2) Four Things Never Satisfied—Using a method of showing that the list is specific, but not exhaustive, and a method of climatic progression, the writer mentions three, yes even four, insatiable things that are never satisfied:

"The leech has two daughters;
  'Give, give,' they cry.
Three things are never satisfied;
  four never say, 'Enough':
Sheol, the barren womb,
  the earth ever thirsty for water,
  and the fire which never says, 'Enough.' " (Proverbs
30:15-16)

Although the meaning of the Hebrew word "leech" *(aluqah)* is uncertain and is found only here in the Old Testament, it is perhaps an Aramaic loan-word[71] for a "leech" or "bloodsucker." It

---

[70]"Visit" carries with it the connotation of "caring for," or "being concerned with," or "supplying the needs of," (*cf* Jeremiah 23:2; Zechariah 11:16; Matthew 25:36, 43).
[71]Francis Brown, S. R. Driver, and Charles Briggs, *A Hebrew and English Lexicon of the Old Testament* (Oxford, 1966), p. 763.

is so translated in the Greek Old Testament (LXX). The Arabians also use this word to refer to a man-eating demon which is insatiable. Whatever the correct rendering of the word, it is used as an illustration of the covetousness of such evil individuals and their distinguishing vices, that of greed and cruelty.

The first insatiable thing is the grave, or Sheol (verse 16). No matter how full the graves become, Sheol is never satisfied as it continues to cry, "More, more." During the Old Testament period of God's history, there was, among the Hebrew people, no definitive concept of life after death. Death was considered an amoral, unconscious Sheol, a shadowy place to which all who die go. It is understandable, therefore, that death was something to be feared. Men were urged to obey God's will and delay their death. Although everyone would ultimately die and go to Sheol, the wise man would live so that he would not die too soon. Thus, death held a sway on the Hebrew people. It was something to be feared, something that was never satisfied, something always seeking another body. This fear has now been transformed into great joy, however, with the advent of Christ who conquered death. God became man in the person of Jesus Christ and we need no longer fear the shadow of death for we have been given victory over death through Jesus Christ.

The second thing never satisfied is the barren womb (verse 16). Chief among the desires of the Hebrew people was the desire for children. Only in bearing children could the Hebrew woman achieve her purpose in life. We see this in Rachel's cry, "Give me children, or I shall die" (Genesis 30:1). The child represented the continuence of the life and character of the parents. As discussed above, with no real concept of immortality, the Hebrew people thought they could live through their descendents. To be without children was not only humiliation and shame (Genesis 16:4), but also sorrow for only through children could there be hope for future life. Then too, children were seen as a sign of God's favor. The Psalmist wrote: "Lo, sons are a heritage from the Lord, the fruit of the womb a reward. . . . Happy is the man who has his quiver full of them!" (Psalm 127:3-5; cf Genesis 16:10; 17:2, 4-5; Exodus 1:7; Psalms 128:3-4). Thus, it is easy to understand why the womb that was barren was continually crying for a child.

The earth ever thirsty for water is the third insatiable thing (verse 16). The soil of Palestine was parched and dry most of the year, and as such, could not be easily satisfied by water. The problem with the land of Israel is not in the annual amount of rain that falls, but in the number of rainy days and in the intensity of rain. The entire annual amount of rain falls in 40 to 60 days in a season of seven to eight months. In dry years this total amount can be greatly reduced, hence the truth that "the earth (is) ever thirsty for water."

Finally, fire is a thing that is never satisfied (verse 16). This verse may refer to the toil required in keeping fuel supplied for an ever-hungry fire, or it may refer to the destruction wrought by an out of control fury.

The purpose of these four insatiable things is to illustrate that man, too, is many times motivated by hopes and desires that are just as insatiable. In the realm of materialism, man devours more and more material things, like the grave, the desert, and the fire devour, yet man's thirst and hunger for more is always present. This is the very theme the Preacher was discussing in Ecclesiastes 2:1-11. Life is more than having joy, pleasure and the material, however. Life can only be complete with the Lord God, or as Augustine says, "Thou madest us for Thyself, and our heart is restless, until it repose in Thee."[72]

(3) Four Things That Are Incomprehensible—It is interesting to note that God turned to the things of nature in order to proclaim his power to Job (Job 38-40) as the writer of Proverbs does here to express his amazement of the things in God's creation. In Job, God raises questions concerning the wonders of nature and God's control of the world to make Job aware of his own ignorance and his folly in arguing against God's wisdom and justice. The wonderful things of the creation and man's inability to understand them and why they exist sufficiently reveals to the man of wisdom that God is at the center of things and not man. The God who made the world is so far above man that it is impossible for man with his limited wisdom to perceive the wisdom of God. God cannot reveal himself completely because man cannot understand God completely. However, even though man cannot understand God, man can trust God. Such trust is based on how God governs his creation.

"The way of an eagle in the sky, the way of a serpent on a rock, the way of a ship on the high seas, and the way of a man with a maiden," are all alike things which created awe within the mind of

---

[72]A. Augustine, op. cit., p. 5.

130

the writer of Proverbs. The fourth thing, "The way of a man with a maiden," parallels a situation within mankind with some marvelous things in nature. According to Scott: "There has been much debate about the meaning of this proverb; is it that in each case there is movement which leaves no trace? (cf Wisdom of Solomon v. 9-12.) Or, that the thing named is without visible means of propulsion? In either case the application to the human situation is problematical. Most think of the last line as a reference to the mystery of the act of procreation (cf the idiom 'he went into her,' Ruth 4:13, etc.); but there are also the attendant mysteries of the attraction of the sexes in general, and of the love of a particular man for a particular woman."[73]

(4) Four Things That Are Intolerable—Utilizing two examples of men and two of women, the wise man speaks about four individuals who manifest qualities that are unberable:

"Under three things the earth trembles;
    under four it cannot bear up:
a slave when he become king,
    and a fool when he is filled with food;
an unloved woman when she gets a husband,
    and a maid when she succeeds her mistress." (Proverbs 30:21-23)

In each of these examples, the illustration points to a situation in which individuals have been raised to a higher rank, or lifestyle, and, as a result, develop superior and arrogant attitudes. The reversal of social order and classes often results in such situations.

The writer of Proverbs has spoken earlier on the dangers of promoting a servant to the position of kingship: "It is not fitting for a fool to live in luxury, much less for a slave to rule over princes" (Proverbs 19:10). We are introduced to the problems that arise when the wrong people are placed in positions for which they are not suited or trained. How great a calamity it is when those who are ruled are placed in a position of ruling. Servants, low in the social scale, would manifest arrogance and insolence toward those above them socially, should these servants be given a position of kingship. The social order would be inverted and oppression would

[73]R.B.Y. Scott, op. cit., p. 181.

follow thus producing an intolerable situation.

A second intolerable thing is "a fool when he is filled with food" (verse 22). This individual has all the abundance of material goods which one could desire. He lives without cares and concerns and, as a result, he lives his life never settling on a purposeful existance with direction and meaning. Such individuals are incapable of real pity or sympathy (sensibility to the needs and concerns of others). They are heartless and arrogant. In their self-centeredness they do not care for the welfare of others.

"An unloved woman when she gets a husband" (verse 23), is the third intolerable thing listed by the writer of Proverbs. The word "unloved" is literally "hated" and might imply that the woman is naturally unpleasant or that she is an old maid who has passed her life without love. Whatever the exact meaning, the writer pictures a woman who is unattractive, ill-tempered and generally repulsive. If such a woman ever does marry, she become unbearable in her new-found position. Scott believes that this phrase, "unloved woman," is a technical term describing one of two wives rejected by her husband and that she is unbearable because she maintains her rights even though she is unloved by her husband (cf Deuteronomy 21:15-17; Genesis 29:30-31).[74]

The final intolerable thing in this list is a maid who has succeeded to the position of her mistress (verse 23). As does the servant promoted to kingship, so the maid promoted to her mistress' position is likewise arrogant and unbearable to those around her. Even though Hagar did not supplant Sarah with Abraham (Genesis 16:1-6), the contempt between the two reveals just how intolerable such a situation might become should it develop in the life of any family.

(5) Four Small But Wise Things—There is inherent in man the tendency to minimize the worth of small things. It is the elephant, not the mouse that gets the attention. From the tower of Babel to the Pyramids of Egypt; from the Collossus of Rhodes to the modern skyscrapers of the United States, bigness has captured the attention and the hearts of men. Contrary to this, the writer of Proverbs emphasizes the importance of small things. As talented and as sophisticated as man is, he can learn from the humble creatures of the earth. Thus four things which, though small, manifest great insight are as follows:

---

[74]Ibid., p. 181.

132

> "Four things on earth are small,
>   but they are exceedingly wise;
> the ants are a people not strong,
>   yet they provide their food in the summer;
> The badgers are a people not mighty,
>   yet they make their homes in the rocks;
> the locust have no king,
>   yet all of them march in rank; the lizard you can take in
>   your hands, yet it is in king's palaces."
>
> (Proverbs 30:24-28)

As noted in Proverbs 6:6, the ant is set up as an example of industry and foresight to the sluggard. They know the time of their opportunity and make the most of it through diligent effort. The rule of life that is wise is one that accepts each day that God gives with joy and thanksgiving and one that does not idle away the time that has been given. The ant redeems the time, needs no prodding, perpares for the future. This is the challenge to man, to be wise like the ant and prepare for the winter of life which God prepared for his people. The apostle Paul gives this advice: "Conduct yourselves wisely toward outsiders, making the most of the time" (Colossians 4:5).

The second small, but wise, thing is the badger (verse 26). The Hebrew term refers to rock-badgers, a species of small mammals about the size of small rabbits. They were very wise creatures in that they realize their feebleness and live in the rocks. Knowing their frailty, they did not trust in their own strength, but fled to a strong place of refuge when danger arose. Thus the wise man is an individual who is aware of the feebleness of his own life and is driven to the strong places of refuge in the land. As the Psalmist writes, "God is our refuge and strength, a very present help in trouble" (Psalms 46:1).

Great wisdom is also manifested by the locusts (verse 27). Although they have no king, they maintain a certain royalty about themselves. Though small and weak, they accomplish wonderful things in the world of nature by working together in unity. They reveal that a life of discipline, direction and order is a life that is able to accomplish great things. The wisdom of co-operation and working together is seen in the work of the locust. The power of such co-operation on the part of the locust is vividly expressed in Joel 2:4-9. How very weak man is when he stands

alone but with the support of his brethren he can withstand mighty
blows. Through unity man can work great works in life.

The final example of a little, but wise, thing is the lizard (verse 28).
By determination and continued effort, this agile and clever little
animal finds his way into the palaces of Eastern monarchs. Here
is an example to nudge the wise individual to persistency. Many
dream magnificent dreams but never wake up and work enough to
make them come true. Some are admirable architects of plans but
are unable to get the plans off paper and into action. The person
who combines dreams, plans and action reaps the reward of bringing
a work, even a life, to completion. The secret of success is not
luck but hard work and perseverence. As the Preacher put it so well,
"In the morning sow your seed, and at evening withhold not your
hand" (Ecclesiastes 11:6).

(6) Four Stately Things—The penman of Proverbs 30 now turns
his attention to four stately, or majestic, things which bring to the
perceptive eye scenes of grandeur and beauty:

"Three things are stately in their tread;
    four are stately in their stride:
the lion which is mightiest among beasts
    and does not turn back before any;
the strutting cock, the he-goat,
    and a king striding before his people." (Proverbs 30:29-31)

Some have interpreted these verses to refer to the arrogance, or
domination, of these various subjects. However, the proverbs writer
has in mind the beauty of the mentioned things with no real
moralizing or philosophizing intended. There is always in man a
sense of awe when he is in the presence of the majestic. Yet, in the
midst of all such majesty, man must continually be reminded, "Only
God is great." And in the midst of all such majesty man must also
be reminded of the words of Jesus: "You know that the rulers of
the Gentiles lord it over them, and their great men exercise authority
over them. It shall not be so among you; but whoever would be
great among you must be your servant, and whoever would be first
among you must be your slave; even as the Son of man came not to
be served but to serve, and to give his life as a ransom for many"
(Matthew 20:25-28). In Christ, God has revealed a new type of
majesty.

Conclusion

The closing words of Agur son of Jakeh of Massa, seem to be fitting words to close this book. In the midst of striving to live godly lives, all men can benefit from Agur's advice:

> "If you have been foolish, exalting yourself,
>   or if you have been devising evil,
>   put your hand on your mouth.
> For pressing milk produces curds,
>   pressing the nose produces blood,
>   and pressing anger produces strife." (Proverbs 30:32-33)

The avoidance of devising evil and producing strife are certainly two of the greatest works that men can engage in today. These two works are so closely aligned with the two great commandments given by Jesus Christ (Matthew 22:37-40). The avoidance of evil reflects a love for God and his will in one's life, and the avoidance of exalting of self and the stirring up of strife through anger, reflects a love for our neighbor and his well being. Truly the wise individual will mold his life around these two principles: "Love the Lord your God with all your heart, and with all your soul, and with all your mind," and "Love your neighbor as yourself."

Bibliography

BOOKS

Adney, W. F. *The Pulpit Commentary,* Vol. 9, Proverbs. Grand Rapids: Eerdmans Publishing Co., 1962.

Aquanias, Thomas. *Basic Writings of Saint Thomas Aquanias.* New York: Random House, 1945.

Augustine, Aureline. *City of God.* tr. Healey, John. New York: E. P. Dutton, 1957.

——————. *The Confessions of Augustine.* tr. Edward B. Pusey. New York: MacMillian Co., 1961.

Churchill, Winston C. *Great Contemporaries.* New York: G. P. Putnam's Sons, 1937.

Clark, Adam. *Clark's Commentary* Vol. 3, *Job-Song of Solomon.* Nashville: Abingdon Press, n.d.

Deane, W. J. and Taylor-Taswell, S. T. *The Pulpit Commentary,* Vol. 9, *Proverbs.* Grand Rapids: Eerdmans Publishing Co., 1962.

Delitzsch, F. *Keil-Delitzsch Commentary on the Old Testament,* Vol. VI, *Proverbs, Ecclesiastes, Song of Solomon.* Grand Rapids: Eerdmans Publishing Co., 1973.

Donne, John. *Devotions,* ed. John Sparrow. London: Cambridge University Press, 1923.

Dixon, W. MacNeile. *The Human Situation.* New York: Longmans, 1937.

Eissfeldt, O. *Kleine Schriften,* I and II.

Fritsch, Charles T. *The Interpreter's Bible,* Vol. 4, *Psalms, Proverbs.* Nashville: Abingdon Press, 1955.

Grenfell, Wilfred. *A Labrador Logbook.* Boston: 1938.

Johnson, E. *The Pulpit Commentary,* Vol. 9, *Proverbs.* Grand Rapids: Eerdmans Publishing Co., 1962.

Kant, Immanuel. *Fundamental Principles of the Metaphysics of*

Morals. tr. T. K. Abbott. London: Longmans, Green and Co., 1909.

Kidner, Derek. *The Proverbs.* Downer's Grove, N.Y.: Inter-Varsity Press, 1978.

Kilpatrick, G. G. D. *The Interpreter's Bible,* Vol. 5, Isaiah. Nashville: Abingdon Press, 1956.

Lewis, C. S. *Mere Christianity.* New York: The MacMillian Co., 1960.

Lindsay, Hal. *The Terminal Generation.* Old Tappan, N.J.: Revell, 1976.

MacCunn, John. *The Making of Character.* New York: The MacMillian Co., 1900.

Reckitt, M. B. *Faith and Society.* New York: 1932.

Rowley, H. H. *Wisdon in Israel and the Ancient Near East.* Atlantic Highlands, N.J.: Humanities Press, Inc., 1960.

Schloerb, Rolland W. *The Interpreter's Bible,* Vol. 4, *Psalms, Proverbs.* Nashville: Abingdon Press, 1955.

Scott, R. B. Y. *The Anchor Bible,* Vol. 18, *Proverbs, Ecclesiastes.* Garden City, N.Y.: Doubleday and Co., Inc., 1965.

Schaeffer, Francis A. *Pollution and the Death of Man, The Christian View of Ecology.* Wheaton, Ill.: Tyndale House Publishers, 1970.

Steere, Douglas V. *Prayer and Worship.* Wallingford, Pa.: Pendle Hill, 1938.

Stevenson, Robert Lewis. *Lay Morals and Other Papers.* New York: Charles Scribner's Sons, 1911.

Taylor, Richard Shelley. *The Disciplined Life.* Minneapolis: Bethany Fellowship, Inc., 1962.

Walton, Izzac. *The Compleat Angler.* Guildford, Surrey, G. B.: Briddles, Ltd., 1962.

Wilson, Herman O. *Studies in Proverbs.* Austin, Texas: Sweet Publishing Co., 1969.

Yutang, Lin. *The Importance of Living.* New York: Reynal and Hitchcock, Inc., 1937.

DICTIONARIES AND ENCYCLOPEDIAS

Blank, S. H. "Proverbs, Book of," *The Interpreter's Dictionary of the Bible,* Vol. 3, 940.

Blank, S. H. "Folly," *The Interpreter's Dictionary of the Bible,* Vol. 2, 304.

Brown, Frances: Driver, S. R. and Briggs, Charles. *A Hebrew and English Lexicon of the Old Testament,* 763.

MAGAZINES

Bryce, Glendon E. "Another Wisdom—'Book' in Proverbs," *Journal of Biblical Literature,* Vol. 91, No. 2 (June, 1972), 145-57.

_____. "Omen-Wisdom in Ancient Israel," *Journal of Biblical Literature,* Vol. 94, No. 1 (March, 1975), 19-37.

Maisel, Albert Q. "Alcohol and Your Brain," *The Reader's Digest* (June, 1970), n.p.

Trible, Phyllis. "Wisdom Builds a Poem: The Architecture of Proverbs 1:20-33, *Journal of Biblical Literature,* Vol. 94, No. 4 (Dec., 1975), 509-18.

Scripture Index

I. OLD TESTAMENT

144